T0271949

Routledge Revivals

Development in Malaysia

The Malaysian economy has grown remarkably since 1970 but despite this poverty is still widespread. This book, first published in 1986, examines the record of economic development in Malaysia over this period and evaluates the success of the New Economic Policy. In particular it examines the merits of the trusteeship strategy in its aim to eradicate poverty and in socio-economic restructuring.

Development in Malaysia

Poverty, Wealth and Trusteeship

Ozay Mehmet

Routledge
Taylor & Francis Group

First published in 1986
by Croom Helm Ltd

This edition first published in 2011 by Routledge
2 Park Square, Milton Park, Abingdon, Oxon, OX14 4RN

Simultaneously published in the USA and Canada
by Routledge
270 Madison Avenue, New York, NY 10016

Routledge is an imprint of the Taylor & Francis Group, an informa business

Publisher's Note
The publisher has gone to great lengths to ensure the quality of this reprint but
points out that some imperfections in the original copies may be apparent.

Disclaimer
The publisher has made every effort to trace copyright holders and welcomes
correspondence from those they have been unable to contact.

A Library of Congress record exists under LC Control Number: 88948918

ISBN 13: 978-0-415-60888-6 (hbk)

DEVELOPMENT IN MALAYSIA

Poverty, Wealth and Trusteeship

OZAY MEHMET

Professor of International Affairs,
Carleton University,
Ottawa, Ont.,
Canada

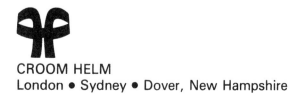

CROOM HELM
London • Sydney • Dover, New Hampshire

© 1986 Ozay Mehmet
Croom Helm Ltd, Provident House, Burrell Row,
Beckenham, Kent BR3 1AT
Croom Helm Australia Pty Ltd, Suite 4, 6th Floor,
64–76 Kippax Street, Surry Hills, NSW 2010, Australia

British Library Cataloguing in Publication Data

Mehmet, Ozay
   Development in Malaysia, poverty, wealth and trusteeship.
   1. Equality — Malaysia   2. Malaysia — Economic conditions
   I. Title
   330.9595′053   HC445.5

   ISBN 0–7099–3525–0

Croom Helm, 51 Washington Street, Dover,
New Hampshire 03820, USA

Library of Congress Cataloging in Publication Data

Mehmet, Ozay.
   Development in Malaysia.

   Includes index.
   1. Income distribution–Malaysia. 2. Malaysia–
economic conditions. 3. Elite (social sciences)–
Malaysia. I. Title.
HC 445 5 79151834   1986   338.9595   85-29079
ISBN 0-7099-3525-0

Phototypeset in English Times by Pat and Anne Murphy
Printed and bound in Great Britain by Mackays of Chatham Ltd, Kent

CONTENTS

To my parents, wife and children

PREFACE

In trying to redress the (racial) imbalance, it will be necessary to concentrate your efforts on the Malays, to bring out more Malay entrepreneurs and to bring out and to make Malay millionaires, if you like, so that the number of Malays who are rich equals the number of Chinese who are rich . . . Mohammed Mahathir, Prime Minister of Malaysia

This study is about the distribution of economic rewards resulting from a rapid process of income growth. Malaysia represents a successful case of a developing country which has achieved an impressive and sustained rate of growth in the last quarter century. This success, however, must be qualified by a failure to eradicate mass poverty and equalise opportunity for all.

The central argument of this study is that the ruling elites, in assuming the role of trustees, have emerged as a cartel. In the process, they have effectively cornered economic planning and decision-making to enrich themselves while paying lip-service to poverty eradication. Inter-racial income inequality, historically a major source of conflict in multi-racial Malaysia, is now being replaced by widening intra-ethnic inequality, especially among the Malays.

Cartels, whether of producers or of ruling elites, possess certain characteristics in common. They have a small membership, and a monopoly over vital information about prices, markets and business opportunities. Members of cartels can strike mutually enriching deals by influence peddling and exchanging vital information unavailable to the general public. Thus, contracts to modernise telecommunications may be awarded to privileged members of ruling elites; foreign investors and multinational corporations seeking approval to go into business may be matched in joint ventures with military or political networks; public enterprises may be 'privatised' by being handed over to private interests linked to the ruling elites. Making millionaires by patronage is not only inconsistent with the rules of fair play; it is also contrary to the rules of economic efficiency in as much as chosen entrepreneurs may mismanage those resources placed under their control.

Preface

Malaysian economic development is a particularly appropriate case to study the effective influence of cartel-like networks over economic planning and policy. Since 1970 Malaysia has adopted a New Economic Policy (NEP) which, as we shall see, is a strategy of development by trusteeship. Two major objectives of the NEP have been: (1) poverty eradication, and (2) socio-economic restructuring. Cartel-like domination of the NEP by interlocking networks of ruling elites has had but a marginal net impact on poverty eradication up to 1983 while concentrating income and wealth among trustees and their associates. This implies that the modalities of distribution of additional income, realised during the successful Malaysian growth performance, can be considered as a Zero-Sum Game in the sense that mass poverty at the bottom is a necessary condition for income and wealth concentration at the top.

The important implication of this analysis is that the presumed conflict between equity and growth is, in reality, a problem of economic exploitation. This is not necessarily class-based exploitation, as Neo-Marxist analysts would argue. More conventionally and simply, it is underpayment of the weaker, the unorganised and the under-privileged by the powerful, the organised and the well-connected. For example, unorganised workers may be exploited in labour markets by cheap labour policies. The underpayment of labour results in quasi-rents as unearned incomes which accrue to members of cartel-like networks.

The roots of economic exploitation in Malaysia lie in colonialism. Many of its instruments, such as a policy of cheap labour, have been left intact by trustees who, in many ways, are successors of the colonial elite.[1] In the colonial era the economic surplus was drained away to London; under post-Independent trusteeship it has tended to enrich the trustees. In a fundamental sense, therefore, persistent poverty in Malaysia stems from the fact that, despite more than 25 years of political independence, the country's economy is still managed in an inherently colonial manner.

This study is undertaken in a positivist, reformist framework. It evaluates the performance of the NEP as a basis for policy options, especially in view of the fact that the NEP time-frame will expire in 1990. Its central theme is that the way to ameliorate poverty is through more competition in markets and more fairness in economic policy. For example, terminating cheap labour policies would end *de facto* colonialism in the plantation sector, expanding the labour share of the national income and helping to alleviate poverty. Fairness in economic policy requires that state assistance should be provided only to those who need it, regardless of race.

One of the most critical preconditions of the transition from a cartel-dominated environment to one of more competition and greater fairness, is information, not only about markets and opportunities, but also about the decision-making process itself. For development projects are approved not only on the basis of technical and economic criteria, but also on what are euphemistically called 'institutional' factors. Paramount among the latter are the key political and bureaucratic decision-makers and a network of influential, special interest groups, which, in Chapter 6, are defined as 'distributional coalitions'. Who make up these networks and coalitions? By what techniques do they seek to influence economic policy and planning to bias the distribution process in their own favour?

The theory of cartels underscores the fact that collusive behaviour requires secrecy and control of information for optimal timing of mutually profitable deals. Therefore, it is not surprising that in studies of economic development, there has been too little attention paid to the control strategies and the inner workings of cartel-like groups and their domination of the growth and distribution process. This study seeks to make a small contribution towards filling this large gap.

Many individuals and institutions have contributed, in various ways, to this study and I wish to record my appreciation to them all. In particular, I would like to express my gratitude to Royal Professor Ungku Aziz, Vice-Chancellor of the University of Malaya, and Professor Yip Yat Hoong, Dean of the Institute of Advanced Studies at that University, for inviting me as a Visiting Professor during 1983/84 which gave me the opportunity to conduct the necessary research for the study. This Visiting Professorship was made possible by a Leave Fellowship granted by the Social Sciences and Humanities Research Council of Canada, which had also provided research grants for field work in Malaysia in 1980 and 1981. I am also grateful to the International Development Research Centre, Ottawa for a research grant through the University of Malaya which financed the survey of 1982/83 graduates reported in Chapter 5. In Malaysia, I wish to record my thanks for help, advice and critical comment to Jomo K. Sundaram, Leo Frederick, Sritua Arief, Rick Shand, Mavis and James Puthucheary, Seih Mei Ling, Paul Chan, S. Husin Ali, R. Thillainathan, Toh Kin Woon, David Gibbons, Abu Asmara, Saleh Kayakoti, A. Navamukundan and Alias Mohammed, among others. I owe a special word of thanks to Koh Kok Eng for computational work. Of course, none can be held accountable in any way for my opinions or interpretations. In Canada, I would like to acknowledge the helpful comments of Martin Rudner, Richard Stubbs, Susan McLellan and my graduate students at the University of Ottawa and Carleton University. Gregg Vaz provided editorial assistance. Last, but not least, I owe my wife and my children a huge debt of gratitude for their tolerance and understanding during the long months of research and writing.

The publication of this study has been assisted financially by the Faculty of Administration and the Institute of International Development and Cooperation, University of Ottawa.

Notes

1. Ozay Mehmet, *Economic Planning and Social Justice in Developing Countries*, Croom Helm, London, 1978, Chapter 5: 'Malaysia: From Colonial to Bumiputera Elitism'.

PART ONE: THE PROBLEM OF POVERTY

1 THE ORIGINS OF ECONOMIC TRUSTEESHIP

Introduction

Malaysia is a resource-rich country. It is the world's leading producer of rubber, palm oil and tin and possesses adequate reserves of oil and gas. It is a relatively small country with a low population density, especially in East Malaysia. Since gaining independence in 1957 it has relied on economic planning. Its aggregate savings have been extremely high, and during 1970–80 its Gross National Product grew at an average rate of 7.8 per cent per annum. As a result of these favourable circumstances, real *per capita* income was 60 per cent higher in 1980 than in 1970 — an average growth rate of 4.9 per cent p.a. (Table 1.1). In 1983 the Malaysia *per capita* GNP, in current prices, was $4,317,[1] or slightly less than US $2,000, second only to that of Singapore in the ASEAN region.

Table 1.1: Principal Macro Indicators Of Malaysian Economic Growth, 1970–1980

Item	1970	1980	Average Annual Growth Rate (%)
1. GNP at purchaser's value (1970 prices in $ mill.)	11,953	25,444	7.8
2. GNP/capita (in 1970 $)	1,109	1,784	4.9
3. Savings (as % of GNP)	21.6	27.2	
4. Gross Investment (as % of GNP)	21.4	29.6	

Source: Items 1. and 2.: 4MP, Table 2.2, p. 17
       Items 3. and 4.: 4MP, Table 2.5, p. 26

The challenge of the Malaysian development policy is not the lack of resources, savings constraint, or the rate of growth of production. It is the distribution of income and wealth. More particularly, the challenge is how to manage the distribution of additional income generated by rapid growth.

Despite the very impressive macro-economic indicators, Malaysia has had a large and stubborn poverty problem. In 1970, one in every two households was officially designated as poor. In absolute

Table 1.2: Trends in Poverty Reduction In Peninsular Malaysia, by Rural-Urban Sectors, 1970–1983 (Figures in Thousands of Households)

(1) Sector	(2) 1970	(3) 1980 Original	(4) 1980 Revised	(5) 1983	(6) Net Change	(7) 1990 Target
Rural	705.9	568.5	542.1	619.7	− 86.2	
Urban	85.9	97.6	93.8	97.7	+ 11.8	
Total	791.8	661.1	635.9	717.6	− 74.2	
Targets		768.3				513.9

Sources: Cols (2) & (3): 4MP, Table 3.2, p. 34
         Cols (4) & (5): MTR4MP, Table 3.2, p. 80
         Targets from 3MP, Table 4.13, p. 73

terms there were 791.8 thousand poor households in Peninsular Malaysia, of which 89 per cent were rural and 11 per cent urban (Table 1.2). In the two of every three rural households that were poor, the incidence of poverty was significantly higher among those Malays who depended on traditional padi cultivation, fishing and small rubber holdings.

The Malaysian poverty problem is not only large, it is very persistent. By 1983, there had been a net reduction of poverty of 74,200 households, 9.4 per cent over a 13-year period. This poor performance took place in a period of rapid economic growth during which numerous programmes were undertaken and large amounts of public funds were spent in a top-down approach to poverty eradication.

Which Development Theory?

The Malaysian poverty problem is of major theoretical interest. The Neo-classical (Trickle-down) theory suggests that the problems of poverty and unequal distribution can be resolved without recourse to special policy interventions by simply accelerating the rate of growth of production. The Malaysian experience tends to disprove this optimistic and overly simplistic theory. This theory assumes perfect competition such that those factors which participate in production are rewarded according to their productivity. In fact, as we shall see in the following pages, planned development in Malaysia — as in the Third World in general — occurs in an environment of market imperfections and economic exploitation. Monopolies and oligopolies dominate markets; government agencies regulate prices; and there is collusion among cartel-like special interests seeking to strike mutually profitable deals. All these imperfections lead to economic exploitation in the sense that some factors are under-compensated for their productivity, while others are over-compensated, deriving quasi-rents as unearned increments of income.

The Malaysian experience suggests a further weakness in the Trickle-down theory: Planned development, as a decision-making process, does not function as an unbiased, impersonal system of resource allocation according to Adam Smith's principle of the Invisible Hand. Rather it parallels decision-making within a cartel. This study will provide ample evidence of this. Thus, the theory of cartels may be a more appropriate theoretical tool to explain the consequences of postwar planning in developing countries. Consequently, questions regarding the identity, motives or behaviour of decision-makers are no less important than are questions concerning aggregate income/output or consumption/saving relationships.

Why is there Persistent Poverty in Malaysia?

Three schools of thought dominate the Malaysian literature on poverty. The Structuralist-Institutionalist school, associated with Ungku Aziz, explains rural Malay poverty in terms of structured monopoly-monopsony exploitation. This system generates excessive profits for middlemen and the impoverishment of the Malay peasants.[2] An important branch of the Structuralist school, the feudal land-ownership theory, is advanced by Syed Husin Ali who attributes rural poverty to the dynamic fragmentation of land resulting from a combination of Islamic inheritance laws and population growth.[3]

The Cultural school explains Malay poverty essentially in terms of Islamic values, particularly those of fatalism, low levels of aspirations and motivation.[4]

More recently a third school of thought, *the Dependency Theory*, has emerged,[5] focusing attention on the international causes of underdevelopment. This school is more an evolutionary than a new theory, building on and extending the work of Emerson, Li, and Puthucheary.[6] According to this school, persistent poverty in Malaysia stems from its unequal and dependent participation in the new international division of labour.

These theories have one common positivist link, that poverty can be cured by policy intervention. If only the right policies were designed (e.g. to eliminate exploitation by middlemen, to reform land tenure or lessen external dependence), the poverty somehow would be reduced. This is an optimistic view, derived from the nineteenth century European liberalism, justifying a top-down bureaucratic strategy whereby the poor passively benefit from policies and services designed and provided for them by well-meaning and enlightened policy-makers.

Development by Trusteeship

How much academic theorising influenced Malaysian development policy is impossible to determine. In May, 1969 there were bloody race riots in Malaysia. This event, known as the *May 13 Incident*,[7] represents a landmark in Malaysian development policy. It directly led to the adoption of the New Economic Policy with a 20-year sunset clause which will expire in 1990.

The Malaysian New Economic Policy (NEP) is a unique planning strategy based on development by trusteeship. It has two principal objectives: (1) poverty eradication, and (2) socio-economic restructuring.[8] Evaluating the implementation and performance of these policy objectives is the central task of this study.

What is Development by Trusteeship?

There are two essential features of the Malaysian strategy of NEP trusteeship: (1) decisions about budget and resource allocations and investment priorities are made non-competitively by rules and procedures set by trustees, and (2) control over resources is separated from their ownership, and vested with the trustees.

Who are the trustees? They consist of two groups. At the top is a small group of political decision-makers whose vision and ideas determine the goals and policy objectives. Subordinate to them is a large body of officials and public service staff who act as intermediaries implementing, executing and monitoring the various programmes and projects designed under the trusteeship.

Development by trusteeship differs, fundamentally, from a competitive system. In a competitive economy resources are allocated according to the rules of supply and demand, and economic rewards, as factor shares, are determined on the basis of productive participation in the production system. Under a system of development by trusteeship, wealth distribution and poverty incidence significantly depend on the trustees' decisions and the manner in which those decisions are implemented. If those decisions are efficient and equitable, then both the production and distribution objectives of development may be promoted in a more effective manner than under a capitalist or the socialist system.

The Overall Purpose

The overall purpose of this study is to evaluate the performance of the Malaysian strategy of development by trusteeship in order to identify the underlying reasons for its success or failure in eradicating poverty and inequality. Does it represent a viable alternative to the Western development model? Or is it an artificial formula of elite control of the development process?

The Emergence of the Malaysian Trusteeship Strategy

How did the Malaysian trusteeship strategy come about? What are its historical and institutional roots? In this introductory chapter we deal with these questions in an effort to provide a historical perspective to the analysis in the following chapters.

In Malaysia, economic activity has traditionally been identified with race.[9] The colonial interests controlled the plantations, banking, finance and public administration.[10] The Chinese and Indians, originally imported as cheap labour for tin mines and plantations, gradually emerged as the dominant groups in the modern sectors. In the process of developing the colonial economy, the Malays were left dependent on subsistence peasant agriculture. As a by-product of this historical process, the Malaysian economy has been burdened by a legacy of fragmented organisation. For example, the labour market has been characterised by ethnic fragmentation[11] in which large and persistent racial wage differentials prevail, in addition to differences by skill, sex and regions.[12]

Under the NEP trusteeship, the Malaysian government has established a 20-year time frame to equalise economic opportunity for all citizens by eliminating the identification of economic function with race.[13] To achieve this, the NEP was designed to give effect to the special rights and privileges of the Malays under the Constitution[14] by initiating a variety of protective policies. These include subsidies, quotas, scholarships and licensing and trade concessions, in order to offset the Malays' historical disadvantage in relation to other races. As a policy package this amounts to a

Malaysian version of an *Affirmative Action Programme.* Since it
deals with economic development, it could more appropriately be
considered as a race-based *Infant Industry Argument.*

NEP as an Infant Industry Argument

The case for protective policies as a development strategy is neither
new nor unique to Malaysia. It has a long history in economic
literature and has a powerful theoretical basis known as the Infant
Industry Argument. It has been, in varying degrees, the guiding
principle of much of the postwar industrialisation policy of
developing countries. It was originally developed by the German
economist Frederich List[15] whose theories very much influenced
Bismarck's policies of industrial development. List was an
economic nationalist whose theory, the opposite of the Free Trade
theory of David Ricardo, was designed to justify the application of
protective tariffs and subsidies to domestic industries which, in
their early stages of development, could not compete with the more
established foreign producers who would flood the domestic
market with cheaper products, thereby effectively and permanently
preventing local industrial development. In the course of time, the
argument ran, these local industries would become efficient enough
to achieve international competitiveness, at which time the need for
protection would be eliminated.

Subsequently, Allyn Young extended the theoretical basis of the
Infant Industry Argument with his theory of growth with increasing returns to scale.[16] Young argued that as new industries matured
and expanded their operations towards an optimally efficient scale,
their average unit costs would decline progressively since fixed costs
would be spread over an increasing output and productivity gains
would result from learning by doing, specialisation and worker
dexterity.

The Malays' 'special rights', a colonial legacy enshrined in the
Constitution and made the corner-stone of the NEP, can appropriately be described and analysed as a special application of the
Infant Industry Argument. The basic rationale of the NEP is to
raise the economic position of the Malay, relative to non-Malays,
by a policy of positive discrimination. Just as domestic infant
industries may require protective tariffs and subsidiaries so, under
the NEP, Malays are granted state subsidies, favourable treatment
under licensing and franchising regulations, quotas in jobs and
university places, concessional loans and grants to enter industry

and trade and privileged access to capital markets in line with the policy target of equity restructuring.

Historically, the Malays always looked to their rulers and government as *the protector*.[17] The *rakyat* (i.e. the subject masses) gave their rulers total loyalty and obedience and expected wardship in return. Colonial rule did little to change this feudal, patron-client relationship. In the first dozen years after Independence increasingly it appeared to the *rakyat* that their historical protection was being eroded by the policy of the gradual accommo-dation of the non-Malay races. The race-riots of May 1969 effec-tively arrested this trend of accommodation. The NEP, which directly followed these riots, restored the historical role of the state as the protector of the *rakyat*, providing a political as well as an expanding economic security net.

Bureacratic Expansion under the NEP Trusteeship

The major impact of the NEP trusteeship has been to legitimise the growth of a large bureaucracy to manage and monitor the new Malaysian state capitalism. Table 1.3 summarises the growth of the federal public service establishment during the period 1970−83. These data refer only to posts for which monies have been approved and allocated in the regular budget. They include unfilled vacancies as well as posts that are actually staffed. The establishment is

Table 1.3: The Growth Of The Federal Public Service[a] 1970−1983

Category[b]	1970 No.	1970 %	1983 No.	1983 %	Change 1970−83 No.	Change 1970−83 %
I (A)	8,091	5.80	52,137	9.99	44,046	11.52
II (B)	6,869	4.93	34,090	6.53	27,221	7.12
III (C)	59,178	42.43	209,065	40.06	149,887	39.20
IV (D)	37,561	26.93	226,188	43.35	188,627	49.33
Others	20,835	14.94	338	0.07	− 20,497	− 5.36
Not Stated	6,933	4.97	−	−	− 6,933	− 1.81
Total	139,467	100.00	521,818	100.00	382,351	100.00

Notes: a. Excludes the Armed Forces and Police.
b. Categories I, II, III, IV (for 1970) are comparable to the 1983 system of A, B, C, D

Sources: Malaysia: *The Expenditure Budget of the Federal Government*, Govern-ment Printer, Kuala Lumpur, 1970; Malaysia: *Anggaran Belanjawan Program dan Prestasi*, Kuala Lumpur, 1984

partial and underestimates the size and growth of the NEP trusteeship bureaucracy after 1970. State civil service and local
government agencies are excluded as are the numerous public enterprises and other Off Budget Agencies (OBAs). The data also
exclude members of the armed forces and the police.

During 1970–83 there was almost a four-fold expansion of the
federal public service. It rose from 139,467 in 1970 to 521,818 at the
end of 1983. While, numerically, some of the largest expansions
were in such areas as education and health services, the most
dramatic rates of growth were in statutory bodies specifically set up
or expanded to implement the rural development and poverty
eradication programmes of the NEP trusteeship. For example, the
National Padi and Rice Authority's (Lembaga Padi dan Beras
Negara, LPN) establishment rose from a mere 29 in 1970 to 4,974
by 1983; the Federal Land Consolidation and Rehabilitation
Authority's (FELCRA) size went up from 136 to 2,900; the Federal
Land Development Authority (FELDA) experienced a fourfold
expansion, increasing to 8,590. Several new agencies were created
or revamped out of earlier, much smaller ones: the Rubber
Industry Smallholders Development Authority (RISDA) had an
establishment size of 5,768 by 1983, the Farmer Organisations'
Authority (FOA) 2,797, the Agricultural Bank of Malaysia (Bank
Pertanian Malaysia BPM) 1,667 and the Malaysian Agriculture
Research and Development Institute (MARDI) 4,601.

The public service establishment is divided into four main categories: I, II, III, and IV subsequently changed to A, B, C, D. The
most rapid growth occurred in the senior category I, entry into
which normally requires a university degree; hence the great
emphasis on paper qualifications and university expansion under
the NEP. This subject will be further discussed in Chapter 5.

Public Enterprises. Another branch of the bureacracy which
experienced rapid growth under the trusteeship system was the
public enterprise sector. During this period various special-purpose
state enterprises, outside the normal public service, were created.
This sector included banks and financial institutions (e.g. Bank
Bumiputera), Bumiputera companies in every major sector of the
economy (PERNAS, PETRONAS, MISC, MAS), and various
joint-venture enterprises. Owing to the lack of comprehensive published statistics on these enterprises, partly due to the fragmented
and uncoordinated nature of their management and operation,

only incomplete data exist to document their rate and pattern of growth, especially regarding employment. In 1974 a Ministry of Public Enterprises was established, not to control, but to coordinate, the functions, not of all, but certain agencies (e.g. SEDCs) placed under its jurisdiction. No central authority has overall control over the extensive public enterprise sector. Its growth under the NEP trusteeship can only be pieced together from various secondary sources. According to one source[18] at the end of December 1974, there were 45 public enterprises owned by the federal government in addition to 37 state-owned public enterprises. By the end of the 1970s, there were 91 federal public enterprises and 56 state statutory bodies.[19] The functions and roles of several of these bodies and agencies will be examined in the following chapters.

However, before proceeding further, it should be mentioned that there are also conceptual and operational difficulties in classifying these public enterprises, whether done on the basis of function or organisational structure,[20] or from the standpoint of accountability and performance. The objective however, is not to dwell on these complex issues, but to highlight the rapid expansion of a top-heavy bureaucracy which directly followed the NEP trusteeship strategy, ostensibly to spearhead and accelerate the participation of Malays in the modern sector.

Poverty Trends under Trusteeship, 1970–83

What has been the impact of the trusteeship system on the problem of poverty in Malaysia?

By 1983, there had been a net reduction in poverty of 74,200 households compared to 1970 (Table 1.2). This represents an overall reduction of 9.4 per cent over a 13 year period. While rural poverty declined by 86,200 households, there were 11,800 more poor households in the urban sector. This evidence gives rise to two questions. First, is a reduction in poverty of 9.4 per cent over 13 years adequate? Second, is there an inter-sectoral poverty transfer process whereby the rural poor are now moving into the urban areas? The latter question will be examined in Chapter 4, while the former will be analysed in detail in Chapters 2 and 3, following an overview presented below.

The original targets of the *Third Malaysia Plan* were that total poverty in Peninsular Malaysia would decline to 768.3 thousand households in 1980, and then to 513.9 thousand by 1990. In other words, the targeted reduction in poverty during 1970–80 was 23.5 thousand households, or an average of 2,400 a year; whereas for the 1980s the targeted annual average was 25,400. The actual reduction during 1970–80 was much higher than expected: a total of 130.7 thousand households were taken off the poverty list, at an annual rate of 13,100. So, up to 1980, poverty redressal policies were ahead of target.

The Malaysian poverty policies took a bad turn after 1980, accountable in part to the world recession and the slumping commodity prices. There was an absolute increase in poverty during 1980–83. By 1983, the poverty redressal policy was already behind target by 25.5 thousand households. This implies that to meet the 1990 target, an average of 29,000 households must be taken out of poverty each year, or the rate of poverty eradication must be increased by 2.5 times relative to the boom period of 1970–80. With the world economic recession still very much a factor, it is safe to conclude that poverty eradication will fall far short of the 1990 target.[21]

The failure of the poverty eradication policies under the NEP trusteeship goes much deeper than the external factor of the world economic recession. In fact, it stems primarily from domestic reasons connected with programme delivery and implementation, the politics of the trusteeship system itself, as well as numerous economic and non-economic factors which will be documented in the following pages.

Outline of the Study

The study consists of four Parts. Following this (Part One) introduction, Part Two will provide a detailed, sectoral profile of the Malaysian poverty problem. Chapters 2 and 3 will analyse rural poverty, the former by examining its incidence and structure, and the latter by evaluating the policy interventions of the NEP intended to redress it. Chapter 4 will examine industrialisation policy and its impact on poverty.

In Part Three we shall focus attention on wealth-concentrating policies under NEP. Chapter 5 will examine mobilisation of aggregate savings and trends in the ownership and control of wealth, specifically of corporate assets under the equity restructuring policy and human capital formation through higher education. Chapter 6 focuses on the rent-seeking behaviour of the Malaysian elites. Finally, Part Four, which consists of Chapter 7, concludes with a summary and discussion of future prospects and policy alternatives.

Notes

1. Malaysia, *Mid-Term Review of the Fourth Malaysia Plan* (hereafter referred to as MTR4MP), Government Printer, Kuala Lumpur, 1984, Table 2.2, p. 44. All dollar amounts in the text are M$ except where specifically stated otherwise.
2. Ungku A. Aziz, 'Poverty and Rural Development in Malaysia', *Kajian Ekonomi Malaysia*, vol. 1, no. 1, June 1964, pp. 70–96. For a recent overview of the poverty literature, see: *Some Case Studies on Poverty in Malaysia, essays presented to Professor Ungku A. Aziz*, edited by B. A. R. Mokhzani and Khoo Siew Mun, Persatuan Ekonomi Malaysia, Kuala Lumpur, 1977.
3. Syed Husin Ali, 'Land Concentration and Poverty among the Rural Malays', *Nusantara*, Bil. 1, January 1972, pp. 100–13. See also Charles Hirschman, 'Sociology' in *Malaysian Studies: Present Knowledge and Research Trends*, edited by John A. Lent, Occasional Paper No. 7, 1979, Centre for Southeast Asian Studies, Northern Illinois University.
4. Brien K. Parkinson, 'Non-economic Factors in the Economic Retardation of the Rural Malays', *Modern Asian Studies*, vol. I, Part 1, January 1967, reprinted in *Readings on Malaysian Economic Development*, edited by David Lim, Oxford University Press, Kuala Lumpur, 1975, pp. 332–40. For a counter-argument, see William Wilder, 'Islam, Other Factors and Malay Backwardness: Comments on an Argument', *Modern Asian Studies*, vol. 2, Part 2, April 1968, and Parkinson's rejoinder in the same volume. These articles are both reprinted in David Lim, pp. 341–9.
5. Khor Kok Peng, *The Malaysian Economy, Structures and Dependence*, Maricans/Institut Masyarakat, Kuala Lumpur, 1983; Ai Yun, 'Capitalist Development, Class and Race' in *Ethnicity, Class and Development, Malaysia*, edited by S. Husin Ali, Persuatan Sains Sosial Malaysia, Kuala Lumpur, 1984, pp. 296–328.
6. Rupert Emerson, *Malaysia: A Study in Direct and Indirect Rule*, Macmillan, London, 1937; Li Dun Jen, *The Economic Development of Modern Malaya*, Oxford University Press, Kuala Lumpur, 1967; J. J. Puthucheary, *Ownership and Control in the Malayan Economy*, Eastern Universities Press, Singapore, 1960.
7. J. Slimming, *Malaysia: Death of a Democracy*, John Murray, London, 1969; Karl von Vorys, *Democracy without Consensus, Communalism and Political Stability in Malaysia*, Princeton University Press, Princeton, N.J., 1975.
8. Malaysia, *Third Malaysia Plan 1976–1980* (hereafter referred to as 3MP or TMP), Government Printer, Kuala Lumpur, 1976, para. 27, p. 7.
9. Ibid.
10. See for example, Douglas S. Pauuw and John C. H. Fei, *The Transition in Open Dualistic Economy, Theory and Southeast Asian Experience*, Yale University Press, New Haven, 1973.
11. Ozay Mehmet, 'Manpower Planning and Labour Markets in Developing Countries: A Case Study of West Malaysia', *Journal of Development Studies*, vol. 8, no. 2, 1971, pp. 277–89.
12. See, for example, the data in Ministry of Labour and Manpower, *Occupational Wage Surveys* (various issues), Kuala Lumpur.
13. TMP, para. 28, p. 7. A historical study of the emergence of the NEP is given in R. Thillainathan, *An Analysis of the Effects of Policies for the Redistribution of*

Income and Wealth in West Malaysia, 1957–75, unpublished Ph.D. Thesis, London School of Economics, University of London, 1976.

14. Art. 153 as amended in 1971.

15. Frederich List, *The National System of Political Economy*, A. M. Kelley, New York, 1966.

16. Allyn Young, 'Increasing Returns and Economic Progress', *Economic Journal*, vol. 58, 1928, pp. 527–42.

17. Chandra Muzaffar, *Protector? An analysis of the concept and practice of loyalty in leader-led relationships within Malay Society*, Aliran, 1979. Also, see S. Husin Ali, *The Malays, Their Problems and Future*, Heinemann Selangor, Malaysia, 1981, esp. Ch. 3.

18. Raja Mohd. Affandi bin Raja Halim, 'Coordination of Public Enterprises: Country Study for Malaysia' in *Public Enterprise in Asia: Coordination and Control*, edited by Abu Sharaf H. K. Sadique, Asian Centre for Development Administration, Kuala Lumpur, Malaysia, 1974, p. 366.

19. Bruce Gale, *Politics and Public Enterprise in Malaysia*, Eastern Universities Press Sdn Bhd, Singapore 1981, Appendix 4, pp. 224–8. See also, R. Thillainathan, 'Malaysia' in *The Role of Public Enterprise in National Development in Southeast Asia: Problems and Prospects*, edited by Nguyen Truong, RIHED, Singapore, 1976.

20. For a recent discussion of these subjects, see Mavis Puthucheary, 'The Political Economy of Public Enterprises in Malaysia', in *The Malaysian Economy at the Crossroads: Policy Adjustment or Structural Transformation*, edited by Lim Lin Lean and Chee Peng Lim, Malaysian Economic Association, Kuala Lumpur, 1984, pp. 217–35.

21. This has now been officially recognised. See the *Mid-Term Review of the Fourth Malaysia Plan*, para. 14, p. 7. But the blame is placed on external factors due to the global economic recession.

PART TWO: POVERTY REPRODUCTION UNDER THE NEP

2 THE STRUCTURE AND INCIDENCE OF RURAL POVERTY IN MALAYSIA

Introduction

In Malaysian Development Plans, agricultural and rural development have consistently been assigned high priority in the allocation of public expenditures. In the Second Malaysia Plan of 1971–75, 24.2 per cent of the total revised planned expenditure was allocated to agriculture and rural development. In the Third Malaysia Plan of 1976–80, this proportion was 23.6 per cent, and declined slightly to 19.6 per cent under the Fourth Malaysia Plan, 1981–85 (Table 2.1). However, in the latest Mid-Term Review of the Fourth Malaysia Plan, there was a sharp relative decline in line with the new National Agricultural Policy which tends to de-emphasise subsidies in general.[1]

Within the agricultural and rural sectors, top priority has consistently been placed on land development and settlement, principally implemented through the Federal Land Development Authority (FELDA). Land development and settlement is essentially a strategy of expansion and replanting within Malaysia's vast rubber and oil palm plantation sector. Within the agriculture and rural development budget of the Fourth Malaysia Plan, the share of funds allocated to land development and replanting represented about 50 per cent of the total development budget, compared to 57.4 per cent and 60.9 per cent under the Third and Second Plans respectively (Table 2.1).

The second major component of agricultural and rural development strategy is associated with the policy objective of achieving rice self-sufficiency. Influenced by the technology of the Green Revolution, extensive drainage and irrigation works have been undertaken, financed by the World Bank, as part of an effort to modernise and commercialise padi cultivation.

Since 1970, following the adoption of the NEP trusteeship strategy, the eradication of rural poverty has become an explicit objective of rural development policy by promoting higher incomes and productivity in agriculture which traditionally has contained high incidence of poverty.

17

Table 2.1: Allocation of Development Budget for Agriculture and Rural Development, under the Malaysian Plan (in millions of $)

Item	1971–75 SMP (Revised) (1)	%	1976–80 TMP (Rev) (2)	%	FMP (Original) (3)	%	1981–83 FMP (Rev) (4)	%
Agriculture and rural development	$2,368.96	100.0	$7,585.23	100.0	$8,359.10	100.0	$7,985.95	100.0
of which Rubber replanting	190.16	8.0	636.54	8.4	316.66	3.8	479.36	6.0
Land development	1,252.73	52.9	3,715.47	49.0	3,732.57	44.7	3,542.70	44.4
D.I.D.	314.21	13.3	828.86	10.9	860.33	10.3	1,487.46	18.6
Agric. credits marketing	179.52	7.6	843.11	11.1	761.32	9.1	584.34	7.3
Others	432.34	18.2	1,561.32	20.6	2,688.22	32.1	1,892.09	23.7
Total plan budget	10,255.45	100.0	32,075.68	100.0	42,859.50	100.0	59,669.38	100.0
Agriculture and rural dev share (%)		23.1		23.6		19.5		13.4

Sources: Col. (1): TMP, Table 12.3, pp. 240–1
Col. (2): MTR3MP, Appendix I
Col. (3) and (4): MTR4MP, Appendix A

Chapter Outline

The purpose of this chapter is to document and analyse the structure of persistent poverty in rural Malaysia. It provides a background to the next chapter, which will be concerned with the effectiveness of policy interventions designed and implemented to redress poverty. First, poverty will be examined in the plantation sector, highlighting the paradox that, while this sector is still the backbone of the economy, it nevertheless accounts for the highest concentration of poverty. This phenomenon will be explored with reference to the estate and rubber smallholding sectors. Subsequently, structural poverty among padi farmers, the second largest concentration of poverty in Malaysia will be studied.

The next chapter will briefly examine the third area of significant poverty incidence — viz. fisheries — in the context of anti-poverty policy interventions. Smaller poverty groups, such as the coconut smallholders and the *Orang Asli* will not be considered since the aim is not comprehensive coverage but rather a highlighting of the salient features of the Malaysian poverty problem.

Persistent Poverty in the Plantation Sector

Despite rapid industrialisation since Independence in 1957 and the petroleum boom since 1974, Malaysian prosperity is still heavily dependent upon export earnings from rubber, supplemented since 1960, by oil palm.[2] In 1980, when petroleum prices peaked, export earnings from rubber and oil palm accounted for about a quarter of the total gross commodity exports of Malaysia, a proportion which exceeded that of exports of manufactures or of crude petroleum (Table 2.2). In 1983, when rubber prices were extremely low, the share of exports of manufactures and of crude petroleum jumped ahead of the share of exports of rubber and oil palm.

Although plantation crops have been the chief contributors to *national* prosperity, the highest incidence of poverty in Malaysia is found among households dependent upon the main export crop: rubber. Furthermore, this incidence of poverty appears to be extremely persistent, having declined only marginally since 1970, while the country experienced an otherwise impressive growth performance. In 1970, according to official statistics, 38.5 per cent of total poor households in Peninsular Malaysia depended on plantation export crops; by 1983, both the absolute and relative poverty

Table 2.2: Share of Rubber and Oil Palm in Malaysian Export Earnings, 1970–83 (in Millions of $)

Item	1970 $	1970 %	1975 $	1975 %	1980 $	1980 %	1983 $	1983 %
1. Rubber	1,724	33.4	2,026	21.9	4,617	16.4	3,664	11.1
2. Oil palm	264	5.1	1,320	14.3	2,515	8.9	2,977	9.1
Sub-total	1,988	38.5	3,346	36.2	7,132	25.3	6,661	20.2
3. Manufactures	572	11.1	1,927	20.9	6,107	21.7	9,797	29.8
4. Crude petroleum	164	3.2	726	7.9	6,709	23.8	7,871	23.9
5. All other commodities	2,439	47.2	3,232	35.0	8,224	29.2	8,594	26.1
6. Total gross commodity exports	5,163	100.0	9,231	100.0	28,172	100.0	32,923	100.0

Sources: 1970 and 1975 are from 4MP, Table 2.3, pp. 18–19
          1980 and 1983 are from MTR4MP, Table 2.4, pp. 48–9

Table 2.3: Poverty Households in Plantation Agriculture (Figures in Thousands)

Sector	1970 Poverty Households	1970 % of Total	1980 Poverty Households	1980 % of Total	1983 Poverty Households	1983 % of Total
Agriculture of which	582.4	73.6	443.7	66.7	497.6	69.3
Rubber smallholders	226.4	28.6	175.9	26.4	247.9	34.5
Oil palm	2.0	0.3	1.9	0.2	1.5	0.2
Coconut small- holders	16.9	2.1	12.8	1.9	10.1	1.4
Estate workers	59.4	7.5	39.5	5.9	57.7	8.1
Plantations agriculture	304.7	38.5	230.1	34.4	317.2	44.2
Non-Agriculture	209.4	26.4	222.4	33.3	220.0	30.7
Total	791.8	100.0	666.1	100.0	717.6	100.0

Sources: 1970 figures are from 4MP, Table 3.1, p. 33
          1980 and 1983 figures are from MTR4MP, Table 3.2, p. 80

in the plantation sector had increased, in large measure due to the slumping of rubber prices after 1980 (Table 2.3).

National Prosperity and Persistent Poverty on Plantations

The coexistence of national prosperity with persistent poverty in the plantation sector is no mere coincidence. It stems from a deep-rooted functional relationship in the dynamics of the plantation economy which generates both growth and impoverishment as part and parcel of the production and distribution process. The origins of this relationship lie in the colonial cheap labour policy which was intended to reproduce poverty. The system which reproduces poverty simultaneously accumulates surpluses that enrich those who control and regulate the relations of production and distribution. This colonial plantation management system was left intact after Independence and it has been further expanded under the NEP trusteeship system of development.

To explore further the dynamics of growth and impoverishment in the plantation economy, we now concentrate on the structure of rubber production,[3] within a neo-classical dualist framework: (a) large plantations, or estates, which were originally developed by foreign (mostly British) companies, which still maintain a dominant control; and (b) the rubber smallholdings operated as peasant family enterprises. Historically,[4] the origins of rubber smallholding reflected the demand by Malaysian peasantry for a stake in the enormous wealth siphoned from the country by foreign interests since the beginning of the twentieth century. It is a history of undiminished 'land hunger'[5] in the face of strong resistance by estate interests and colonial authorities.[6] In the postwar period the production share of smallholders has risen quite sharply while that of the estates has declined. In 1981, the smallholders produced 60.6 per cent of total rubber in Peninsular Malaysia compared with 47.6 per cent in 1972 and 41.5 per cent in 1960.[7] Despite the increasing relative importance of the smallholding sector, in 1980 no less than 41.3 per cent of the households in this sector were officially poor.[8] Furthermore, it appears that smallholders' poverty exists amidst general prosperity since as much as 80 per cent of the 1980 output of smallholders originated in six states (Johore, Perak, Negri Sembilan, Pahang, Kedah and Perlis) which, with the exception of the last two, are the relatively high average income states.[9]

Estates and smallholding sectors differ from each other not only in size[10] but in almost every other respect including technology, management, marketing and economic organisation. In the postwar period, especially after Independence, there has been a rapid restructuring of estates. This is reflected by a steady decline in employment as a result of the introduction of labour-saving techniques and increasing conversion to oil palm. Consequently, there has been a substantial rise in labour productivity: during 1960–81,

Table 2.4: Basic Trends in Rubber Estates in Peninsular Malaysia (1960—81)

	Employment ('000) Tappers	Total	Area under Mature Rubber ('000 ha)	Output per Tapper (kg)	Average Tapper Real wage/day ($)	Price RSS 1 f.o.b. (cents/kg)
1960	186.8	285.3	568.7	2247	3.40	238.25
1961	185.1	285.6	557.3	2352	2.81	184.25
1962	185.5	286.2	552.4	2401	2.80	172.50
1963	187.0	286.3	533.1	2490	2.77	159.75
1964	178.5	275.4	548.4	2714	3.07	150.25
1965	181.8	270.1	544.5	2744	3.07	154.50
1966	164.7	249.5	543.3	3170	3.50	144.25
1967	157.3	231.9	544.9	3396	3.50	119.25
1968	145.9	206.7	545.7	3921	3.71	117.00
1969	152.4	215.1	551.7	3956	4.02	154.00
1970	160.1	226.4	544.7	3879	3.95	124.50
1971	137.3	198.7	533.9	4818	3.21	101.75
1972	138.7	196.3	522.1	4754	3.20	93.50
1973	132.4	191.7	508.0	5088	3.41	165.50
1974	138.4	208.3	490.1	4765	3.70	179.50
1975	124.1	187.2	472.4	4680	2.99	136.75
1976	124.0	178.9	462.2	5256	4.40	199.00
1977	120.3	175.0	451.9	5217	3.49	202.75
1978	123.0	177.3	442.4	5024	3.82	229.99
1979	116.8	170.7	433.1	5199	4.40	279.41
1980	114.7	167.2	423.0	5116	4.27	312.25
1981 (July 31)	113.0	164.6	416.7	5083	3.37	257.82

Note: Real wages for 1960—78 are from James Nayagam and Abdullah bin Sapien. Other years have been computed by deflating the money wages from the *Handbook* with the Consumer Price Index from *Bank Negara Quarterly Economic Bulletin*, June 1983, Table vii.8, p. 78

Sources: Malaysia, Dept. of Statistics: *Rubber Statistics Handbook* (several issues) Rubber Research Institute of Malaysia, *Labour Situation in Rubber Estates and Smallholdings* by James Nayagam and Abdullah bin Sapien, Kuala Lumpur, September 1981

output per estate worker increased 2.25 times (Table 2.4).

Who has benefited from these large productivity gains? Recent evidence from the Rubber Research Institute of Malaysia (RRIM), indicates that profit margins can be as high as 55 per cent of gross revenue per kg. (Table 2.5). These margins refer to 'well-organised estates in the size group below 200 planted hectares' or medium-

Table 2.5: Profit Margins in Estates,[a] 1975–81

Item	Cents/kg	%
Total revenue[b]	153.0	100.0
Expenditure		
Management	8.4	5.5
Other overheads	6.5	4.2
Fixed maintenance	11.3	7.4
Latex collection and transport	1.5	1.0
Tapping wages	42.1	27.5
Sub-total	69.8	45.6
Net Profit	83.2	54.4

Notes:
a. Average adopted from nine to seventeen well-organised estates in the size group of below 200 planted hectares surveyed by RRIM Costing and Management Study Group.
b. Net of manufacturing cost, export duty and research cess.

Source: Arrifin bin Mohd. Nor and James Nayagam, 'Incentive Wage Concept: An alternative strategy for land development schemes', *RRIM Preprint #5*, October 1983, Table 5, p. 12.

sized estates. It can be assumed that profit margins on larger estates, where even greater economies of scale exist, would be no less.

Despite large productivity gains and profit margins, estates have one important feature in common with the smallholding sector: *persistent poverty* (Table 2.3). Why should this be so? At first sight, it would be tempting to attribute it to race, since, after all, Malaysia is a multi-racial society and estate labour has, for historical reasons, been largely Indian. But this is incorrect since the vast majority of poor rubber smallholders are Malay. In fact, two sets of parallel explanations are called for, one applicable to the estates, the other to smallholders, although, ultimately, elite management and exploitation emerge as the common, principal explanatory variable.

Poverty on Estates: The Continuing Cheap Labour Policy

During 1960–81, the daily real earnings of tappers did not reflect the big productivity improvement noted above (Table 2.4). In fact, the evidence shows that real wages of tappers actually declined from $3.40 to $3.37 during 1960–81, or remained virtually constant if an average of 1980–81 is taken in view of the fact that

Table 2.6: Average Comparison of Monthly Earnings[a] of Estate Tappers and Manufacturing Workers, 1967 and 1981

	1967	June 1981
	$	$
1. Average monthly earnings of estate tapper[b]	87.50	147.40
2. Average monthly earnings of manufacturing worker[c]	166.40	430.44
3. Ratio of 2.:1.	1.90	2.92

Notes:
a. in money terms
b. This figure is computed as the product of the daily wage of $3.50 ($6.70 in 1981) and 25 tapping days (22 in 1981)
c. The 1967 earnings are deflated back from June 1973 using the Consumer Price Index

Sources:
1. Dept. of Statistics, *Rubber Statistics Handbook*
2. Dept. of Statistics, *Monthly Industries Statistics of West Malaysia* (June 1981 and 1973)

1981 was a poor year. However, the same data show that there has been a substantial decline in the ratio of wages to gross revenue: in 1967 this ratio was 25 per cent, but it declined to 14 per cent in 1981.[11] Furthermore, the wage differential between estate tappers and manufacturing workers widened further during 1967–81, jumping from 1.90 to 2.92 (Table 2.6).

Wages on rubber estates are linked to movements in the price of rubber (f.o.b. RSS 1) which, as can be seen from the last column in Table 2.4, is subject to large and severe fluctuations. While producers can cushion themselves against these fluctuations by stockpiling and other forms of supply management, the estate workers have no such protection. The agreement between the Malaysian Agricultural Producers Association (MAPA) and the National Union of Plantation Workers (NUPW) is deficient in several important respects. In the first place, it assumes that there is a direct and immediate linkage between rubber prices and rates of pay of estate workers. This is not the case because of stockpiling by producers and consumers abroad and the lagged transmission mechanism in the supply/demand relationship. It is not irrelevant to observe that, for example, the wages of tyre industry workers in industrialised countries are not similarly linked to rubber price fluctuations. The effect of direct linkage is to pass the deflationary consequences of price swings onto the estate workers and undermine their economic welfare. Another deficiency of the MAPA-NUPW agreements stems from the delays in reaching these accords. For example, the last agreement negotiated at the end of 1979 provided for a basic wage of $4.30, up from $3.60 in the 1976 agreement — i.e. an increase of 19.4 per cent. During the period 1976–80 (that is, by the time the 1979 agreement went into effect), the official cost of living index had increased by 21.5 per cent so that the nominal gain in the basic wage negotiated in the new agreement was more than totally nullified.[12] Furthermore, these agreements are exceedingly complex, linking rates of pay not only to rubber prices, but also to the expected yield of trees, terrain and other working conditions, in what at first sight might appear to be a reasonable attempt at matching pay and productivity. In fact, however, they provide the producers with large discretionary powers enabling them to dominate estate workers since they ultimately determine tasks and other working conditions of the workers. Thus, the MAPA-NUPW agreements effectively place estate workers and their rates of pay at the mercy of producers.

In recent years estates have complained of increasing labour shortages,[13] despite falling real wages as noted above, and the fact that money wages for tappers have actually declined from $7.20 a day in 1979 to $6.70 in 1981.[14] As a result, there has been a growing volume of imported Indonesian labour employed on estates at what amounts to poverty-level wages. These Indonesian immigrants are obtained through illegal or quasi-legal channels organised by labour contractors and syndicates, under conditions which are reminiscent of the exploitative colonial labour policies.[15] According to the NUPW sources, in 1981 there were an estimated 130,000 Indonesian estate workers in Peninsular Malaysia, about half of the total estate work-force. The average daily wage of these was about $6, about 90 per cent of the normal wage, and as much as 50 per cent of their earnings was skimmed off by their sponsoring contractors. Typically, Indonesian immigrant estate workers would work under these exploitative conditions for one year, by which time they tended to become familiar enough to find their way to higher-paying construction jobs and hawking in urban informal sectors, ultimately seeking to gain status as Bumiputera citizens.

Under normal competitive conditions, the employers' reaction to genuine labour shortage is to raise money wages and, over time, real wages in order to induce an additional inflow of labour into the sector. The wage data presented above, and in particular, in

Table 2.6, clearly show that this has not happened on the Malaysian rubber estates. Recent reliance on imported Indonesian labour, which has been officially endorsed by the Malaysian government under a 'guest worker scheme',[16] has effectively arrested any upward rise in estate earnings or any narrowing of inter-sectoral wage differentials which otherwise might have occurred.

Employer and official resistance to higher wages on rubber estates discloses a deliberate policy of continuing the traditional cheap labour policy inherited from colonial times. This, in fact, is the basic cause of persistent poverty on the Malaysian estates. From a poverty-redressal policy perspective, reliance on imported cheap labour is self-defeating since it tends to reproduce poverty, contrary to the NEP objective of reducing and eliminating it.

A Poverty Reproduction Model

For this reason, it is important to explore analytically the mechanism by which poverty is reproduced on estates by means of a cheap labour policy and imported Indonesian labour. This is done in Figure 2.1. Panel (a) depicts an initial equilibrium point in the estates labour market, $E°$, at poverty-level income, PLI. The constant PLI reflects the empirically observed trend of real wages, as discussed above and shown in Table 2.4. The total workforce, L, consists of two parts: OL, which refers to resident, Malaysian workers, and $L_r - L_t$ referring to the immigrant workforce. In the absence of Indonesian in-migration, the labour supply schedule in the estates labour market would be $S'_r S'_r$ and given labour demand DD, real wages would tend to increase toward the new equilibrium point E'. Such an increase in real wages would indeed represent poverty reduction on estates. However, the inflow of immigrant workers willing to accept employment at PLI wages enlarges the labour supply to $S'_t S'_t$ and reproduces additional poor households equal to $L_r - L_t$.

Panels (b) and (c) illustrate the shorter-term dynamics of how this poverty reproduction results within a two sector labour market framework. Panel (b) refers to the modern, higher-wage manufacturing/urban sector while panel (c) refers to the plantation sector. Higher wages in the former, denoted by W_1 generate a 'pull' force and an out-migration of resident workers, who have greater mobility. On the basis of this inter-sectoral mobility, *ceteris paribus*, the wage differential would gradually decline from

Figure 2.1: A Poverty Reproduction Model

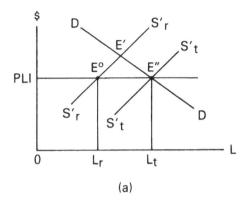

(a)

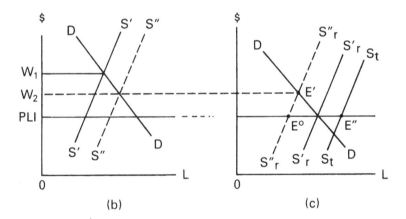

(b)   (c)

$(W_1 - PLI)$ toward equalisation of wages at W_2. In Panel (c) the resident labour supply schedule would shift upwards to $S''_r \ S''_r$ while in Panel (b) supply would expand to $S''S''$.

This wage equalisation process, however, is effectively arrested by Indonesian immigration. The immigrant workers actually provide cheap 'replacement' labour for the resident plantation workers moving from the estates sector. Thus, the actual labour supply schedule in Panel (c) is not $S''_r \ S''_r$ but S_tS_t. The new point of equilibrium is E'' on PLI, not E' at the higher real wage. In this manner, the Malaysian plantations continue to utilise a cheap labour policy while reproducing poverty.

Since the Malaysian government has recently adopted an expansionist population policy under its '70 million' target,[17] the above model of poverty reproduction is of long-term relevance. Reliance on immigration from Indonesia may well be one important means of increasing Malaysia's population. This, however, will tend to reproduce poverty in the country.

The above model may be regarded as too neo-classical, based on unrealistic assumptions such as perfect mobility of labour, rational migration behaviour, and so on. In actual fact, living and working conditions on Malaysian estates are dominated by what amounts to cultural entrapment,[18] where a host of institutional factors impair mobility and patterns of rational behaviour. These institutional factors will be briefly surveyed by focusing on the quality of life of estate workers, in order to supplement the abstract neo-classical model presented above.

The Quality of Life of the Estate Workers

In theory, employers provide estate workers with housing and other fringe benefits. These facilities are supposed to be inspected regularly by the officials of the Ministry of Labour to ensure adequacy and compliance. In actual fact, however, the quality of life of the estate workers has continually deteriorated, as the following brief account will demonstrate.

Housing. Estate houses, which are provided by employers for regular workers, are as small as 130 square feet in area, and may accommodate as many as 8 persons. The space consists of one room, measuring roughly 10ft × 8ft, a small hall and a tiny kitchen 3ft × 6ft. Under Malaysian law, the minimum living space for a household with a maximum of five individuals is 260 sq.ft., at least double the size of estate houses. Overcrowding, however, is not the sole dimension of substandard housing on estates. There is either no electricity supplied at all or, where provided, it is irregular, being available only for a few hours in the early morning or evening. There is no piped water, and 10–15 households have to share a standpipe that supplies water for only a few hours a day. Sometimes families are able to get water only on alternate days while, on some estates, wells are the only source of water. Whether it comes through standpipes or wells, the quality of water is inferior to that supplied to urban populations. In addition estate houses lack toilets, and 20−30 households have to share about 8 pits or bucket latrines. By the end of the day the buckets or pits are full, not only polluting the air but also creating a permanent health hazard.[19]

Nurseries and Education. Although the law regulating working conditions on estates provides for compulsory nurseries or creches for working mothers, these facilities are badly run and exceedingly overcrowded, with 25−30 infants per amah. The substandard nurseries or creches lead to inferior primary schooling on estates. The majority of the children of estate households attend the Tamil schools located on the estates. Not only are the students enrolled in these schools intellectually the most deprived, owing to lack of parental stimulus at home, but the estate schools are, by official recognition, the poorest in the entire educational system.[20] Many schools lack even such basic facilities as a proper building or class-room, toilets, libraries and playing fields. Some of these schools are abandoned rubber smoke-houses, annexes to temples or other dilapidated buildings. Typically, estate schools are single-teacher, multi-class institutions, and the qualifications of teachers are inferior, as is their pay, to those in other levels of Malaysian educa-tion. Under these circumstances, it is not surprising that the Tamil estate schools have the highest drop-out rates, and the lowest achievement levels as compared with other types of primary schools.[21]

Food and Nutrition. In a recent study of the state of food, nutrition and health in plantations,[22] it was found that the diets were inadequate in calories, protein, calcium, iron and carbohydrates, derived from rice, and that sundries (beverages, alcohol, sugar, etc.) provided the bulk of the calories. Rice and sundry items were consumed daily, but meat once a week or less; and eggs and fish once or twice a week. The drinking of alcoholic beverages was widespread among the adults. Overall, the nutrient intakes were below the recommended national allowances of calories, protein, calcium, iron and vitamin B2.

Conclusion

The inferior quality of life among estate workers, caused and reinforced by declining real wages, has been a major determinant of the attrition of labour from the estates. Rather than attempting to improve the quality of life, the official reaction of producers and the government has been to provide additional cheap labour from Indonesia under a 'guest worker scheme'. This scheme, however, tends to reproduce poverty and casts serious doubt upon the commitment of the NEP trustees to poverty eradication.

Rubber Smallholders: Structural Poverty Trap

The highest incidence of poverty in Malaysia is in the rubber small-holding sector. It affects primarily rural Malays, and it is a *structural* problem, both in terms of cause and ultimate remedy. Fundamentally, it stems from the uneconomic size of the holdings, especially in relation to household size. This situation, in turn, is linked causally to multiple-ownership and subdivision, sanctioned under the Islamic law of inheritance. In recent years this has given rise to a growing problem of absentee-ownership further reducing the productive use of cooperant resources. These structural constraints are aggravated cyclically by fluctuations in the world commodity prices affecting the economic welfare of smallholders, estate workers and FELDA settlers.

The latest evidence,[23] analysed below, tends to demonstrate that the smallholder, especially the 'hard-core', is very much an optimiser efficiently using land, labour and working capital at his disposal, to achieve yields per unit of land which are comparable to, or even superior to those achieved on estates. Therefore, his ability to break out of the poverty trap is primarily a function of restructuring land ownership through reform and consolidation. Unfortunately, the Malaysian authorities have resisted land reform, emphasising instead various interventions such as subsidies and extension services, which reflect the dubious assumption that smallholder poverty can be alleviated under the existing structure of land ownership. This official position continues to be the basis of the latest National Agricultural Policy, announced in 1984, which avoids land reform but emphasises the cooperative use of smallholdings.

Identifying Rubber Smallholders

Officially any rubber holding less than 100 acres is defined as a smallholding. However, *de facto*[24] smallholders are difficult to define and count owing to multiple-ownership, idle rubber land owned by absentee owners and difficulties relating to registration of title. Therefore it is not surprising that substantial discrepancies exist between different official agencies regarding the number of rubber smallholders and the incidence of poverty among them. In the Mid-Term Review of the Third Malaysia Plan, the total number of rubber smallholders in 1977 was set at 412,600[25] of whom 198,000, or 48.1 per cent, were deemed to be below the poverty line of income. On the other hand, the figures produced by the Rubber Industry Smallholders' Development Authority (RISDA) census of smallholders are much higher. The total number of rubber small-holders in 1977 was found to be 490,460 of whom 62.1 per cent were considered to be poor.[26] In the analysis below we shall utilise the RISDA data simply because they are a richer source of data which allow a detailed profiling of the rubber smallholders and their poverty.

Socio-economic Profile of Rubber Smallholders

According to the 1977 RISDA census, the average size per holding of the estimated 490,460 smallholders was 2.36 hectares, with a limited range of variation among the 10 states in Peninsular Malaysia.[27] Johore had the largest absolute number of rubber smallholders as well as area devoted to rubber smallholding, followed by Perak, Kelantan, and Kedah/Perlis.

Inter-ethnic variations in the average size per holding were larger than inter-state variations. The Bumiputera had the smallest average holding at 2.0 hectares, the Chinese the largest at 3.49 hectares. Indians had 2.95 and others had 2.31 hectares.[28]

Even sharper inter-ethnic differences are revealed from a comparison of the size distribution of rubber smallholdings. The major fact is that there is a significantly higher incidence of small-holdings among the Malays than non-Malays. Thus, no less than 59.3 per cent of the Bumiputera smallholdings were under 2 hectares, whereas the percentage for the Chinese was 29.9 per cent, for the Indians 40.4 per cent and 54.7 per cent for others.[29]

The average household size and age were significantly higher than the national averages. While there was no significant inter-ethnic variation around the average age of 48.2 years for small-holders, the reverse was the case with the average household size. Surprisingly, the Chinese rubber smallholding households were reported to have an average size of 8.1 persons, or 1.56 times larger than the national average for Peninsular Malaysia.[30]

Table 2.7: Poverty Incidence Among Rubber Smallholders, by Race, 1977

Monthly Household Income/cap.	Bumiputera		Chinese		Indian		Others		Total	
	No.	%	No.	%	No.	%	No.	%	No.	%
$1–19	50,941	13.9	10,670	9.3	893	14.5	669	16.2	63,118	12.9
%		80.7		16.9		1.3		1.1		100.0
20–45	188,505	51.5	48,044	41.9	2,921	50.6	2,061	49.8	241,531	49.2
%		78.0		19.9		1.2		0.9		100.0
Total Poverty Household[a]	239,446	65.4	58,714	51.2	3,760	65.1	2,730	66.0	304,649	62.1
%		78.6		19.3		1.2		0.9		100.0
40–60	40,706	11.1	17,700	15.4	746	12.9	415	10.0	59,567	12.1
%		68.3		29.7		1.3		0.7		100.0
61–79	41,407	11.3	13,413	11.7	470	8.2	487	17.8	55,777	11.4
%		74.2		24.0		0.9		0.9		100.0
80+	44,191	12.2	24,941	21.7	795	13.8	504	12.2	70,431	14.4
%		62.7		35.4		1.2		0.7		100.0
Total	365,750	100.0	114,768	100.0	5,770	100.0	4,136	100.0	490,424[b]	100.0
%		74.6		23.4		1.2		0.8		100.0

Notes: a. Based on a poverty-line income of $45 *per capita* per month, ie $225/month for an average-sized rural household of five persons. See Young, *et al.* (1980), p. 116.
b. This count excludes 36 Indian smallholders in Perlis for whom no information on income was available.

Source: RISDA (1983), Draft Final Report, Kuala Lumpur, Table 3.1(a), p. 91.

The Incidence and Intensity of Poverty

According to the RISDA census, 62.1 per cent of rubber small-holder households in 1977 were in poverty, defined as *per capita* household income of less than $45 per month or $225 per month for an average-sized rural household of 5 persons (Table 2.7). The choice of the $45 cut-off level was based on the assumptions and calculations previously made by the World Bank team of Young, *et al*.[31] This team raised the poverty-line in 1978 from the previous figure of $25 to $33 in 1970 prices. Thus, at the 1970–76 annual rate of increase of 6.7 per cent in the consumer price index, the figure of $33 in 1970 prices is converted into $45 in 1977 prices.

The choice of the particular poverty-line income undoubtedly makes a great difference in the absolute number of poor house-holds, and hence it is not surprising that discrepancies abound in the Malaysian studies of poverty incidence. This difficulty is compounded by the fact that the Malaysian Development Plans have not explicitly indicated the poverty-level incomes that the planners have used in reporting changes over time in the extent of poverty incidence. What is beyond dispute is the fact that poverty incidence is highest among the Bumiputera rubber smallholders, followed by Indians, and least among the Chinese. In addition, as revealed by Table 2.8, the intensity of poverty is highest among the Bumiputera.

The RISDA census measured intensity of poverty among small-holders on the basis of (a) hard-core poor and (b) moderately poor. The former, representing the poorest of the poor, were defined as those households owning less than 0.4 hectares of rubber land *per capita* and having only one agricultural occupation (i.e. either rubber smallholding or other agricultural occupation but no non-agricultural occupation). On the other hand, the moderately poor were defined as households owning less than 0.4 hectares of rubber land and having two agricultural occupations consisting of rubber smallholding and another agricultural occupation, but no non-agricultural occupation. They were also defined as those who owned between 0.41 and 0.60 hectares of rubber land *per capita* and had either one or two agricultural occupations but no non-agricultural occupation. The hard-core households' mean monthly *per capita* income was $31.72, which equalled exactly the Bumiputera figure, whereas the moderately poor households' average was $36.94 (Table 2.8).

Table 2.8: Mean *Per Capita* Total Monthly Household Income and Productivity by Poverty Status and Race, 1977

Poverty Status	Bumiputera		Chinese		Indian		Others		Total	
	MPCTHI	PR	MPCTHI	PR	MPCTHI	PR	MPCTHI	PR	MPCTHI	PR
Hard-core poor	31.72	98.17	31.78	106.46	30.09	122.86	33.37	108.22	31.72	99.99
Moderately poor	36.01	70.62	42.57	81.87	38.47	59.42	33.67	56.37	36.94	68.82
Total poor	34.22	83.62	35.37	95.71	32.33	81.27	33.59	69.60	34.45	87.41
Non-poor	58.49	61.21	86.15	74.84	63.49	64.18	66.95	73.49	62.35	68.21
Total	46.87	70.48	66.07	80.18	50.46	71.98	47.62	78.90	51.96	75.18

Notes: MPCTHI = Mean Per Capita Total Household Income (in current $)
PR = Productivity (in kilogram/hectare/month)

Source: RISDA (1983), Draft Final Report, Kuala Lumpur, Table 3.2(b) p. 17 and Table 3.10(a) p. 123

Productivity and Income

One of the most important questions regarding poverty among rubber smallholders is whether their poverty stems from their own inefficiency (i.e. is he a sub-optimal producer?), or from structural factors (e.g. size of holding) which cannot be influenced by policy interventions without altering the structure of rubber land ownership. Evidence presented in Table 2.9 shows that the smallholders, especially those in the hard-core poverty group, are relatively as efficient as estates in the class size of 101–500 acres. The moderately poor — i.e. those smallholders having a more diversified pattern of household time allocation — are only about 71 per cent as efficient per acre as the reference estates, but the hard-core poor, who are likely to be totally dependent on rubber smallholding, are slightly more so.[32]

Table 2.9: Productivity of Rubber Smallholders and Estates

Producers	Annual Yield / Acre	
	lbs	%
Smallholders by poverty status		
'Hard-core' poor	1,070	103.1
Moderately poor	737	71.0
Total poverty group	936	90.2
Estates by size — planted acres:		
101–500	1,038	100.0
501–1,000	1,307	125.9
1,000 +	1,449	140.0
Average for all estates	1,343	129.4

Sources: Smallholders data, computed from RISDA (1983), Table 3.10(a) p. 123
Data for estates from the socio-economic research unit, RRIM (1981)

These data are subject to certain limitations which must be noted. They are obtained from different sources: smallholder yields from the RISDA census, and estate yields from RRIM. Furthermore, they refer to different years, the former to 1977, the latter to 1981. Nevertheless, the comparative productivity data tends to disprove the popular misconception that the smallholder is inefficient and his poverty can be eliminated by policy interventions without altering the prevailing system of land ownership. Even if it were assumed that there is a 30 per cent potential for raising the poor smallholders' productivity through more subsidies or extension services under the existing ownership structure, this would be insufficient to lift his income level up to the official poverty-line of $45 *per capita*.

Therefore it follows that the effective remedy for the poverty problem of rubber smallholders requires — not as a sufficient but as a necessary condition — land reform to increase the average size of uneconomic holdings. Of course, this is virtually certain to generate excess labour in the process, which will have to be transferred to more productive employment elsewhere in the economy. The NEP strategy of attempting to alleviate poverty through subsidies and extension services perpetuates smallholder poverty by encouraging entrapment of an excessively high labour-land ratio that minimises *per capita* incomes. A more rational transitional policy would be to protect smallholder incomes against fluctuations in world prices by means of a domestic income stabilisation scheme.

Padi Farmers: Another Case of Structural Poverty

The second largest concentration of poverty in Malaysia is among padi farmers in the rice sector. A quarter of a century of 'Green Revolution' technology, along with heavy infra-structural investments and a wide range of subsidy programmes and extension services, have all failed to alter this fact. As in the case of rubber smallholders, all of these policy interventions were conceived and implemented within the existing socio-economic structure, particularly within the context of the prevailing land owership system, reflecting the official view that rapid economic change was compatible with the traditional *status quo*. In fact, however, the existing system of land ownership is unequal, and the types of policies implemented have actually made it even more so. When there is initial maldistribution of productive asset ownership, it is inevitable that policy interventions that leave the system of ownership intact, will lead to inequality of incomes.

Geographically, padi cultivation in Peninsular Malaysia is concentrated in the 'rice bowl' areas of the Muda plain in Kedah and Perlis (operated by the Muda Agricultural Development Authority — MADA) and the Kemubu region in Kelantan (operated by the Kemubu Agricultural Development Authority — KADA). In 1983, MADA's output represented 65.5 per cent of the total rice

Table 2.10: Size Distribution of Padi Farms, by State in West Malaysia

State	< 1 acre	< 2 acres	< 3 acres	< 4 acres	Average Size (acres)
Johore	5	65	92	95	1.5
Kedah	8	27	46	58	4.0
Kelantan	8	34	66	82	2.3
Malacca	21	53	77	84	2.1
Negri Sembilan	38	74	93	97	1.1
Pahang	16	54	80	91	1.7
Penang	9	40	63	76	2.5
Perak	14	40	59	71	2.6
Perlis	3	14	33	49	4.1
Selangor	3	17	22	62	3.6
Trengganu	14	37	66	77	2.3
West Malaysia	10	33	54	68	3.1

Source: IBRD, 'Problems of Rural Poverty in Malaysia', A Report prepared for the FAO/World Bank Cooperative Program, Rome, February 1975, Table 10, p. 79. Quoted in Toh Kin Woon, *The State in Economic Development: A Case Study of Malaysia's New Economic Policy*, PhD Thesis, University Of Malaya, Kuala Lumpur, 1982, p. 286.

production in Peninsular Malaysia of 1,161,000 tonnes, and KADA's output an additional 7 per cent. Other important rice producing areas are the Province Wellesley, the Krian district in northern Perak, and the Tanjung Karang area in Selangor.

Demographically, padi cultivation is the major source of livelihood for approximately one out of every six agricultural households. In 1980 there were a total of 151,000 padi farming households, compared with 140,000 in 1970.[34] It is a heavily Malay activity, with as many as 95 per cent of padi farmers being Malay. That in 1970 no less than 88.1 per cent of the padi farming households lived in poverty is explained by the uneconomic size of padi farms. According to a FAO-World Bank survey in the mid-1970s, the results of which are tabulated in Table 2.10, 68 per cent of padi farms were less than four acres, 54 per cent less than three acres, 33 per cent less than two acres, and 10 per cent were less than one acre.

Despite these structural constraints, the Malaysian government's rice policy has been shaped by a target of self-sufficiency within the existing system of land-ownership. Large-scale investments in irrigation and drainage works, and subsidy and price support programmes have been justified on the basis of this policy target.

During 1970–80, the self-sufficiency ratio was raised significantly from 78 to 92 per cent, but by 1983 it had fallen to 77.3 per cent.[35]

Trends in Poverty Incidence among Padi Farmers

What has been the impact of the rice policy on the incidence of poverty?

In 1970 a total of 123,400, or 88.1 per cent of the total households in the rice sector were officially in poverty. In 1978 the numbers had fallen to 110,600 or 74 per cent (Table 2.11). The Fourth Malaysia Plan reported that the poverty incidence among padi farmers in 1980 was down to 55.1 per cent as a result of

Table 2.11: Incidence of Poverty in the Rice and Padi Sector

Years	Total households	Poor households in rice and padi	Incidence of poverty	% of total poor households
1970	140.0	123.4	88.1	15.6
1975	148.5	114.3	77.0	13.7
1978	149.5	110.6	74.0	14.3
1980	151.0	83.2	55.1	12.5
1980 (Rev)	145.0	76.4	52.7	12.0
1983	138.9	75.0	54.0	10.5
1990 target	133.1	64.3	48.3	14.0

Source: For 1970, 1975, 1980 and 1990: The Fourth Malaysian Plan, Tables 3.1 and 9.4; for 1978, The Mid-Term Review of the Third Malaysian Plan, Table 2.1. For 1980 (Rev) and 1983: The Mid-Term Review of the Fourth Malaysian Plan, Table 3.2, p. 80.

substantial increases in rice subsidies since 1978, but this 25 per cent poverty reduction in just two years is no more than an optimistic 'guesstimate'. A number of independent studies, to be reviewed below, cast serious doubt about this as well as the prospect of achieving the Fourth Malaysia Plan target of 48.3 per cent poverty incidence in the rice sector by 1990.

In fact, there are three recent independent studies, based on extensive surveys and empirical analysis, which reach highly pessimistic conclusions about poverty trends among padi and rice cultivators. They are: (a) a comprehensive survey conducted by the Centre for Policy Research, Science University, Penang (CPR study); (b) a socio-economic impact study of the Kemubu river irrigation project in Kelantan by R. T. Shand, *et al.*; and (c) a World Bank evaluation study of the Muda and Kemubu schemes.

According to the CPR survey, in the Muda scheme the poverty incidence in 1976 (based on the medium estimate[36]) was 62.7 per cent in the Perlis section of the scheme and 68.6 per cent in the Kedah section. In KADA I and II in Kelantan it was 79 per cent, and in Besut in Pahang it was 69.9 per cent. Thus, by the late 1970s, as many as three out of every four padi households were still in poverty, unable to earn an annual average poverty-level income of $3,100 (in 1978 prices). Moreover, the CPR study concluded that, under the existing institutional socio-economic structure, any further poverty reduction toward the 1990 target was unlikely.[37]

The Shand study found that 'even with double cropping and higher productivity, income from padi by itself enabled very few Kemubu households to reach the current poverty line. On average in 1979/80, it provided only 38 per cent of the 1980 poverty line income per household. . . Clearly, most Kemubu farmers had operational areas of padi that were too small to provide even this minimal living standard from crop production and proceeds.'[38]

The World Bank evaluation study of the major rice schemes in Malaysia is of particular significance since these have been financed largely from its loans. The latest Bank evaluation study of the Muda and Kemubu schemes is extremely pessimistic, in so far as the equity and income distribution effects of these schemes are concerned. It shows that in 1979 the average small tenants and owners had incomes which were 57 and 72 per cent of the official poverty level of income, compared with 54 and 57 per cent in 1966,[39] indicating little improvement over this 13-year period despite the large irrigation investments and the Green Revolution technology. On the other hand, the average owner-operator, and especially the average owner-tenant, achieved major income improvements, thanks to their ability to increase their land holdings at the expense of the small farmers and tenants.[40] As with other independent studies, the World Bank evaluation report concluded that without land reform to correct maldistribution of land ownership it would be practically impossible to eradicate poverty among the padi farmers and prevent maldistribution of income.

Structural and Policy-induced Causes of Padi Poverty

There are two principal causes of persistent poverty among the Malaysian padi farmers; (a) structural, and (b) policy-induced determinants. We shall focus attention here on the structural determinants, postponing policy analysis to the next chapter. However, in passing, it is relevant to point out that reduction in poverty was not the paramount objective of rice policy at the outset, nor was it the concern of the 'Green Revolution' technology package. Rather it was maximisation of rice production and yield rates per unit of land. High yielding seeds, fertilisers, mechanised farming and irrigation works were all designed to expand padi cultivation, encourage double-cropping, and commercialise rice production in order to achieve national self-sufficiency in rice *within the existing structure of land ownership.* In fact, the level of rice self-sufficiency rose significantly from 78 per cent in 1970 to 92 per cent in 1980.[41] But Malaysia is a comparatively high-cost, low-quality producer of rice. Therefore the gain toward self-sufficiency must be weighed against the social costs of attaining this target, not only with reference to the alternative option of greater reliance on cheaper imported rice, but also relative to an alternative (e.g. a more egalitarian) system of land ownership.

The Structure of Land Ownership and Technology

Attempts to graft modern rice farming on to the existing structure of land ownership have had the effect of reproducing poverty through increased landlessness. As noted in the case of rubber smallholders, fragmentation stemmed traditionally from the Islamic law of inheritance which required subdivision of the land of the deceased. Under the 'Green Revolution' the poverty impact was particularly accelerated by a new tenurial pattern whereby tenancy gave way to owner-operator farmers. For example, during 1966 and 1975/76, in the Muda area the percentage of tenants, both as farmers and in terms of area cultivated, declined from about 40 per cent to between 20 and 25 per cent (Table 2.12). On the other hand, in the same period, the share of owner-operators rose quite sharply.

Examining trends in the mean farm sizes shows similar trends towards increased land accumulation on the one hand and fragmentation on the other. For example, looking at a poverty farm size of under 4 relongs[42] shows that the mean size declined from 2.5 relongs in 1966 to 2 relongs in 1975/76, whereas within the largest category of farms the mean size increased from 13.9 relongs to 15.3 relongs. These latter farms accounted for a slightly bigger share of total farm area in 1975/76 than in 1966, while accounting for a smaller percentage of total farms. The exactly opposite trend occurred in the case of poverty farms (Table 2.13). Consequently, in this period, the Gini coefficient of land concentration rose

Table 2.12: Farm Tenure, Muda Irrigation Scheme Area, 1955–1975/1976

Tenurial status of farmer	1966		1972/73		1975/76	
	% Farmers	% Area	% Farmers	% Area	% Farmers	% Area
Owner-operator	44.5	39.5	44.0	43.2	56.1	45.3
Mean farm size	5.0		5.5		4.5	
Tenant	41.4	38.8	37.6	30.3	24.5	22.7
Mean farm size	5.3		4.5		5.2	
Owner-tenant	14.0	21.7	18.5	26.6	19.4	32.0
Mean farm size	8.6		8.0		9.3	
Total	100.0	100.0	100.1	100.1	100.0	100.0
Total farmers	49,772		43,921		61,164	
Total area (relong)	280,980		(801)a (4,549)a 249,432		(45,601)b (256,841)b 344,353	
Mean farm size (relong)	5.6		5.6		5.6	

Notes: a. Sample size
b. Attained sample

Source: D. S. Gibbons, *et al.*, *Land Tenure in the Muda Irrigation Area*, p. 167.

sharply, going from 0.354 to 0.445.[43]

As owners increasingly became operators and the larger land-owners began to accumulate padi lands, marginal households sank further into poverty or joined the ranks of the landless. The law of economies of scale, which is the *raison d'être* of commercialised, mechanised farming, thus had two cardinal effects. On the one hand, it raised the productivity of padi lands and promoted maxi-misation of rice production. On the other hand, it created poverty among small padi farmers and tenants. Under a Darwinian regime of survival of the biggest, the social benefits and costs of moder-nising rice production became polarised, actually encouraging the bigger to become even more so at the expense of the small farmers and tenants in an essentially 'zero-sum game'.[44]

What became of the displaced tenants and dispossessed small farmers? It appears that a good number remained in the local community working as casual and seasonal labourers on the larger

Table 2.13: Size Distribution of Farms, Muda Irrigation Scheme
Area, 1966–1975/1976

Farm Size	1966		1972/73		1975/76	
Category (relong)	% Farms	% Area	% Farms	% Area	% Farms	% Area
Less than 4	38.1	17.3	39.5	16.8	46.7	17.0
Mean Farm Size	2.5	—	2.4	—	2.0	—
4–9.9	46.4	44.9	48.5	52.8	38.9	43.2
Mean Farm Size	5.4	—	6.2	—	6.3	—
More than 10	15.3	37.8	12.0	30.4	14.6	39.8
Mean Farm Size	13.9	—	14.4	—	15.3	—
Totals	100.0	100.0	100.0	100.0	100.0	100.0
Total	(2,441)[a]		(801)[a]		(45,549)[b]	
Farms	49,772		43,921		61,164	
Total Area	(13,914)[a]		(4,549)[a]		(256,930)[b]	
Farmed (relong)	280,980		249,432		344,353	
Mean Farm Size (relong)	5.65		5.68		5.63	
Gini Index	.354		.360		.445	

Notes: a. Sample sizes
       b. Actual numbers interviewed
Source: D. S. Gibbons, *et al.*, *Land Tenure in the Muda Irrigation Area*, pp. 158–9

farms, supplementing their income with seasonal off-farm earnings.[45] In the period after 1976 there was a rapid increase in the cost of living as prices of many basic commodities such as fish, vegetables, sugar and coffee rose sharply. As a result, these rural labourers suffered further deterioration in their living standards.[46] The more fortunate ones, however, became settlers on FELDA or similar land schemes,[47] while an unknown number became production workers in industrial estates and informal sectors, some joining the ranks of the working poor.[48]

Notes

1. Malaysia, *Mid-Term Review of the Fourth Malaysia Plan*, Government Printer, Kuala Lumpur, 1984, paras. 47–50, pp. 17–18. (Hereafter denoted as MTR4MP).

2. For a short discussion of the shift to oil palm, see Donald R. Snodgrass, *Inequality and Economic Development in Malaysia*, Oxford University Press, Kuala Lumpur, 1980, pp. 173–4.

3. Oil palm is excluded as a relatively new crop, while coconut estates share similar problems to rubber smallholders.

4. Lim Teck Ghee, *Peasants and Their Agricultural Economy in Colonial Malaya, 1874–1941*, Oxford University Press, Kuala Lumpur, 1977.

5. Shamsul Bahrin, P. D. A. Perera and Lim Heng Kow, *Land Development and Settlement in Malaysia*, Department of Geography, University of Malaya, 1979. For a concise account, see M. Rudner, 'The Malaysian Quandary: Rural Development Policy under the First and Second Five Year Plans' in *Readings on Malaysian Economic Development*, edited by David Lim, Oxford University Press, Kuala Lumpur, 1975.

6. P. T. Bauer, *The Rubber Industry*, Longmans, London, 1948.

7. Malaysia, *Rubber Statistics Handbook*, Dept. of Statistics, Kuala Lumpur (several issues).

8. 4MP, Table 3.1, p. 33.

9. Ibid., Table 5.3, p. 102.

10. Officially, anyone who owns rubber land of less than 41 hectares (i.e. 100 acres) is defined as a 'smallholder'. See *Rubber Statistics Handbook*. The most recent and comprehensive study of the rubber industry is by Colin Barlow: *The Natural Rubber Industry: Its Development, Technology and Economy in Malaysia*, Oxford University Press, Kuala Lumpur, 1978.

11. Calculated in current prices using the following formula:

$$W/GR = dw \times N \times 12/(Qt \times P)$$

where W = annual wages, GR = gross revenue, dw = average daily wage of a tapper ($3.50 in 1967, $6.70 in 1981), N = number of tapping days (25 in 1967, 22 in 1981), Qt = output/tapper (as per Table 2.4), and P = price of RSS[1], fob, in $/kg. Source: same as Table 2.4.

12. The provisions of the last agreement are given in RRIM, *Rubber Owners' Manual* (2nd edn.), Kuala Lumpur, 1983, Ch. 10.

13. James Nagayam and Abdullah bin Sepien, *Labour Situations in Rubber Estates and Smallholdings*, The Rubber Research Institute of Malaysia (RRIM), Kuala Lumpur, September 1981.

14. These money wage-rates, referring to July in each year, are taken from the *Rubber Statistics Handbook*.

15. J. N. Parmer, *Colonial Labour Policy and Administration: A History of Labour in the Rubber Plantation Industry in Malaya, c. 1910–41*, J. J. Augustin, New York, 1960; R. N. Jackson, *Immigrant Labour and the Development of Malaya*, Government Press, Kuala Lumpur, 1961.

In the summer of 1983, a labour contracting scandal was exposed on the FELDA Selanchar Empat scheme, whereby illegal immigrants and other non-status workers were forced to work under near-slavery conditions. See 'Times Focus: Contract Labour', *Malaysia New Straits Times*, 12 July 1983, p. 2.

16. 'Accord with Indons on Travel and Work', *Malaysia New Sunday Times*, 13 May 1984.

17. MTR4MP, para. 59, pp. 21–2.

18. T. Marimuthu, 'Schooling as a Dead End: Education for the Poor especially the Estate Children' in *Ethnicity, Class and Development: Malaysia*, edited by S. Husin Ali, Persatuan Sains Sosial Malaysia, Kuala Lumpur, 1984.

19. Consumer Association of Penang, 'The Forgotten Workers' *Utusan Konsumer*, November 1983, p. 7.

20. T. Marimuthu, 'Schooling as a Dead-End'.

21. 'The Problems with Tamil Schools', *Malaysia New Straits Times*, 10 November 1983.

22. N. Chandrasekharan and T. Marimuthu, 'An inquiry into the State of Food, Nutrition and Health in Plantations', *Medical Journal of Malaysia*, vol. XXXIV, no. 3, 1980, pp. 226–9.

23. RISDA: *Laporan Sementara Banci Pekebun Kecil Getah Semenanjung Malaysia 1977: Analisa Profail Sosio-Ekonomi Kemiskinan dan Penyertaan Dalam Rancangan*, RISDA, Kuala Lumpur, November 1982 (Interim Report); Idem., *Laporan Akhir Banci Pekebun Kecil Getah Semenanjung Malaysia 1977: Analisa Profail Sosio-Ekonomi Kemiskinan dan Penyertaan Dalam Rancangan*, RISDA (Draft Final Report), Kuala Lumpur, August 1983.

24. Barlow, *The Natural Rubber Industry*, p. 229.

25. Malaysia, *Mid-Term Review of the Third Malaysia Plan*, Government Printer, Kuala Lumpur, 1979, p. 28.

26. RISDA, Draft Final Report.

27. Ibid., Table 1.1., p. 7.

28. Ibid., Table 2.23, p. 57.

29. Ibid., Table 2.23, p. 57.

30. Ibid., Table 2.15, p. 45.

31. Kevin Young *et al., Growth and Equity in a Multiracial Society*, World Bank/Johns Hopkins University Press, Baltimore, 1980, p. 116.

32. The data for the reference estates are from the Socio-Economic Research Unit of the Rubber Research Institute of Malaysia.

33. Malaysia, Ministry of Finance, *Economic Report 1983/84*, Government Printer, Kuala Lumpur, 1983, p. 116.

34. 4MP, Table 3.1, p. 33.

35. Malaysia, Ministry of Finance, *Economic Report 1983/84*, p. 105.

36. Sukor Kasim, *et al., Final Report, Study of Strategy, Impact and Future Development of Integrated Agricultural Development Projects* (2 vols.), Pusat Penyelidikan Dasar, Universiti Sains Malaysia, Penang, March 1983, vol. II: Appendix Table 3.1(a).

37. Ibid., vol. I: Main Report, p. v.

38. Richard T. Shand, *et al., Socio-economic Study of the Impact of the Kemubu Irrigation Project in Kelantan, Malaysia*, Universiti Pertanian Malaysia, Serdang, Selangor, March 1982, pp. 472–3.

39. World Bank: *Impact Evaluation Report Malaysia: Muda and Kemubu Irrigation Projects*, Report No. 3587, Washington, D.C., 24 August 1981, p. 26.

40. Ibid., pp. v–vi and Table 4, p. 17.

41. 4MP, para. 699, p. 277.

42. One relong is approximately equal to 1.4 acres. The choice of 4 relongs as the cutoff point is based on S. Jegatheesan, *The Green Revolution and the Muda Irrigation Scheme*, Telok Chengai, Alor Setar, Muda Monograph #30, 1977, quoted in D. S. Gibbons, *et al., Land Tenure in the Muda Irrigation Area: Final Report: Part 2: Findings*, Centre for Policy Research, Universiti Sains Malaysia, Penang, 1982, p. 152.

43. D. S. Gibbons, *Land Tenure*, Table 77, p. 158.

44. This, of course, is a general trend observed elsewhere in the developing countries which have experienced Green Revolution technology. See, for example, K. Griffin, *The Political Economy of Agrarian Change: An Essay on the Green Revolution*, Macmillan, London, 1974.

45. Sukor Kasim, *et al., Final Report, Study of Strategy*, vol. I, pp. 44–6.

46. D. S. Gibbons, *et al., Land Tenure*, p. 180.

47. See Ch. 3, pp. 62–70.

48. Richard T. Shand and Mohd. Ariff Hussein, *A Socio-economic Analysis of the Kemubu Project, Part II*, Universiti Pertanian Malaysia, January 1983, Ch. 6.

3 RURAL POVERTY AND POLICY INTERVENTIONS UNDER TRUSTEESHIP

Introduction

The architects of the strategy of Malaysian rural poverty redressal have chosen to ignore the structural determinants of the problem. Instead, they have equated rural poverty with low productivity, choosing to regard it primarily as a technical problem stemming from imperfections in economic organisation, reinforced by traditional values. More specifically, the policy-makers have been conditioned by a deep-seated conviction that rural farmers and producers have traditionally been at the mercy of the middlemen extracting excessive margins in what Ungku Aziz has called the 'monopoly-monopsony exploitation'.[1] Thus, it was felt that the padi farmers were victimised under the *padi kunca* credit system which, effectively, led to their perpetual indebtedness.[2] The rubber smallholders were similarly exploited by unscrupulous dealers cheating with weights and grading as well as pricing.[3] In the fishing industry the traditional system of fixed profit-sharing was always subject to abuse by boat-owners at the expense of the crew.[4]

Accordingly, in the post-Merdeka period, and especially since 1970 under the NEP trusteeship, a *top-down* interventionist strategy was adopted, focused on the following three policy instruments: (a) institution-building, (b) fiscal policy management featuring large-scale subsidy programmes, and (c) a major programme of land development and settlement. These three instruments will be reviewed and evaluated in terms of their effectiveness in the redressal of rural poverty.

Institution-building at the Centre

In line with the dominant post-war strategy of growth, the Malaysian rural development policy was based solidly on the presumption that the rural poor were too under-educated and backward to make rational choices. Therefore, the vicious circle of poverty in which they were entrapped could only be broken by an

46

enlightened leadership. This presumption, on which the NEP trusteeship system was built, resulted in the creation of a large bureaucracy at the centre managing an institutionalised, top-heavy delivery system. Of course, the Malaysian approach to rural development has traditionally been top-down, stemming from the paternalistic nature of the ruler-ruled relationship among the Malays.[5] Thus, such agencies as the Department of Agriculture and the Ministry of Rural Development, along with numerous other bodies involved in rural development, devoted as much attention to politicising the peasants as to programme delivery.[6] However, this heavily political-bureaucratic process of fighting rural poverty was particularly accelerated after the race riots in May 1969[7] which led to the adoption of the NEP, with poverty redressal as one of the two main objectives of development policy.[8]

A few illustrative examples of institution building under the NEP trusteeship may briefly be listed.

In 1970 the Agricultural Bank of Malaysia (Bank Pertanian Malaysia — BPM) was established with the aim of providing agricultural loans and credit. These were channelled through a network of Farmer Associations, started by the Ministry of Agriculture and modelled on the Taiwanese experience.[9] During 1971–80, a total of $642 million loans was approved by BPM, mainly for padi production and tobacco production and marketing.

In 1971 the National Padi and Rice Authority (Lembaga Padi dan Beras Negara — LPN) was established to manage the Guaranteed Minimum Price (GMP) system of rice price support, to buy padi from farmers, license private buyers and millers, and manage a buffer stock scheme. A more detailed analysis of the LPN will be presented shortly.[10]

In the area of marketing, the Federal Agricultural Marketing Authority (FAMA), originally set up in 1965 with comprehensive and ambitious objectives, was reorganised in the early 1970s into more of an advisory service agency disseminating market information. Its tasks in the marketing of padi and rice, livestock, and fish products were transferred to new agencies such as the LPN, the National Livestock Development Authority (MAJUTERNAK) — subsequently closed down for mismanagement — and the Fisheries Development Authority (MAJUIKAN).

As far as the rubber smallholders were concerned, a Rubber Industry Smallholders' Development Authority (RISDA) was established in 1972 administering a replanting subsidy scheme.

This scheme was financed from the export duty collected by the Malaysian Rubber Exchange and Licensing Board. RISDA also started a network of group processing centres for standardising the processing of field latex into sheet rubber.[11] RISDA's replanting scheme will be examined further presently.[12]

In 1973 a Farmers' Organisation Authority (FOA) was created and given the overall responsibility of organising and increasing the productivity of farmers producing crops other than rubber and oil palm. It was conceived as the key implementing organ of the Integrated Agricultural Development Programme (IADP) linked with the *in situ* development strategy.[13] FOA was based on the theoretically sound premise that farmers' participation at the grass-roots is essential for a successful policy of rural poverty redressal. Thus, FAO was entrusted with the task of institution-building in IADP areas through the creation of farmers' organisations. In addition it had other functions, including the channelling of farm credit, distributing fertiliser subsidies, providing extension service in processing and marketing, integrating farmer organisations and cooperatives and generally assisting in the process of modernising farm management techniques.

In the area of land development and settlement, the principal agency — the Federal Land Development Authority (FELDA), originally established in 1956[14] — was expanded and given a much more activist mandate after 1969. Its work was complemented by the establishment of the Federal Land Consolidation and Rehabilitation Authority (FELCRA) and numerous other state and federal agencies. FELDA's operations will be discussed in some detail in the last part of this chapter.

Bureaucratisation of the Rural Poverty Strategy

Some of the salient features of the top-heavy and top-down strategy of rural poverty strategy will now be highlighted.

Shortage of Bumiputera Manpower. The immediate and short-term impact of the creation of numerous statutory bodies, and the expansion of already existing agencies to design and implement anti-poverty policies was, of course, a sudden shortage of Bumiputera manpower needed to staff all the new vacancies. This, in turn, resulted in a major expansion of public expenditure for higher education and government scholarships to develop the necessary manpower, justified on the basis of the employment restructuring objectives of the NEP.[15]

Early manpower shortages resulted in the adoption of some self-defeating measures by newly-formed statutory bodies anxious to pursue the task of programme implementation. Inexperienced officers were entrusted with multi-million dollar subsidy programmes. In some cases, quite paradoxically, 'foxes' were recruited to guard the chicken. For example, the LPN opted for the appointment of agents from among private mill-owners and rice dealers in rural areas — i.e. precisely the sorts of intermediaries that the LPN was supposed to regulate. Gradually, the inherent weaknesses of the agency system became obvious as large-scale diversions of padi to unlicensed mills took place through the instrumentality of these agents who were over-invoicing actual deliveries and over-claiming their commissions.[16]

Monopolistic Programme Delivery. In the rush to create new institutions at the centre, little attention was given to effective coordination or to mapping out exclusive functional areas of jurisdiction. Whenever there were overlapping terms of reference, each agency adopted an exclusive or monopolistic delivery strategy, competing with and duplicating the work of other related agencies. Thus, RISDA's group processing centres often found themselves encroached upon by the buying activities of the Malaysian Rubber Development Corporation (MARDEC).[17] FELDA, FELCRA and a host of other land development agencies competed for land and settlers,[18] while numerous agencies duplicated each other in the fields of credits, subsidies and scholarships.

One of the most notable examples of waste resulting from monopolistic programme delivery was the activities of the FOA. Established under the Farmers' Organisation Act of 1973, FOA had two main objectives: (a) to promote a network of farmers' associations in IADP areas, and (b) to channel all essential inputs, subsidies and services in the processing and marketing of farm products. With such a wide range of activities, FOA found itself in competition with half a dozen other agencies with similar assignments, including the Department of Agriculture, RISDA, FELCRA and IADP project offices both on site and at regional levels.[19] While the FOA has been reasonably successful in establishing over 200 Farmers' Organisations (FOs) in IADP areas, these have, in turn, attempted to monopolise the delivery of fertiliser and other subsidised inputs, farm credit as well as marketing functions. By so doing, they not only reduced competition but also helped to institutionalise the power of rural elites who emerged as the controlling interests of these organisations.

Politicisation of Grass-roots. The FOs gradually emerged as institutions serving the interests of the richer and more powerful rural elites, including the large land-owners and politicians. These dominant groups have successfully manipulated subsidies and other extension services to their own advantage at the expense of the peasants and poor farmers. The Bank Rakyat scandal,[20] has demonstrated that even the top state politicians have been involved in corrupt and fraudulent practices. In the Muda scheme, according to a recent World Bank study, where 40 per cent of all padi farmers were members of FOs, large farmers who owned more than 7 acres accounted for less than 15 per cent of total farms in the scheme. They were over-represented with more than 25 per cent of the membership and received over 30 per cent of the farm credits (Table 3.1). On the other hand, poor padi farmers with less than 2.84 acres, accounting for almost half the farm area, had a membership share of only 12.4 per cent and a farm credit share of just 6 per cent. One key explanation for this unequal pattern of membership lies in FO's entrance fee, which was previously $3 but was subsequently increased to a hefty $30–100, effectively excluding most of the poor padi farmers.[21]

Malaysia has a long history of politicising rural development.[22] What is unique is that since 1970, under the NEP trusteeship, politicisation has been given official sanction and has been

Table 3.1: Membership in Farmer Organisations and Credit Recipients in the Muda Scheme, by Farm Size

Farm size (Acres)	% of Farms in Muda	% of Farmers who are members	% of Farmer recipients
0.1 –2.84	46.7	12.4	6.0
2.85–5.6	30.6	40.4	34.8
5.7 –7.09	8.3	21.8	29.2
>7.1	14.5	25.4	30.3

Source: World Bank, Quoted in *Final Report: Study of Strategy, Impact and Future Development of Integrated Agricultural Development Projects*, Vol. 1, by S. Kasim, *et al.*, Centre for Policy Research, Universiti Sains Malaysia, Penang, March 1983, p. 79.

institutionalised within the entire spectrum of the fight against rural poverty. Not only is the distribution of farm subsidies and credits ultimately based on political connections and considerations but so are settler selections for FELDA and similar schemes, housing allocations, jobs and scholarships and other government benefits. All of which implies that the way out of poverty for the rural poor is more through political sponsorship and patronage than productivity and hard work. However, the ruling elites manipulated these policies less for promoting efficiency and equity than for political survival.

Fiscal Policy and Rural Poverty

Some of the most important causes of persistent poverty in Malaysia stem from the policy mismanagement of subsidy programmes and tax discrimination against smallholders. In the following pages, these fiscal policy inefficiencies in fisheries, rubber smallholding and padi farming will be examined.

Failure of the Fishery Subsidies

The incidence of poverty among fishermen is heavily concentrated in the East Coast of Peninsular Malaysia, where fishing households are almost entirely Malay (Table 3.2). The reduction of poverty

Table 3.2: Number of Registered Fishermen and Boats by Area and Race in Peninsular Malaysia, 1981

	West Coast	East Coast	Total
Fishermen:			
Malay	26,388	28,150	54,538
Chinese	28,331	1,753	30,084
Indian	609	—	609
Others	1,669	25	1,694
Total	56,997	29,928	86,925
Fishing Boats:			
Inboard	12,472	6,113	18,585
Outboard	6,429	939	7,368
Non-powered	2,948	1,489	4,437
Total	21,849	8,541	30,390

Source: *Annual Fisheries Statistics, 1981*, Fisheries Division, Ministry of Agriculture, November 1982, p. 9.

Table 3.3: Fishermen's Subsidy Scheme, Peninsular Malaysia
(1981–85)

Type of aid	Components of aid provided	Total subsidy ($)
Loans and subsidies for the outfitting of new fishing vessels.	1. Subsidy up to 75% of cost for new engines up to 30 hp. 2. Subsidy up to 100% for engines between 5–8 hp. 3. Subsidy up to a maximum of $1,500 for gear. 4. Loan up to 100% of cost for building boat hulls.	30,000,000
Subsidies for the improvement of existing vessels	1. Subsidy up to 75% of cost of replacing inboard engines. 2. Subsidy up to a maximum of $1,500 for replacing gear. 3. Subsidy up to 100% for providing outboard engines to non-motorised vessels.	10,600,000 1,408,000
Subsidies for nets	1. Subsidy up to 100% for boat owner who does his own fishing.	8,767,500
Subsidies for insulated ice boxes	1. Subsidy of $50 per box (4 boxes for each boat)	3,222,500

Source: Division of Fisheries, Ministry of Agriculture, Kuala Lumpur, 1981

reported in the Fourth Malaysia Plan, from 73.2 per cent in 1970 to 45.3 per cent in 1980, has been almost exclusively due to the introduction of commercial and modern fishing technology, especially trawling and purse-seining, in the Chinese fishing communities on the West Coast where the majority of the fishermen are non-Malay (Table 3.2). The incidence of poverty on the East Coast has remained persistent, as high as 95 per cent according to one estimate.[23]

Under the NEP trusteeship, poverty-reducing policies have focused on the Malay fishermen on the East Coast and have taken the form of all kinds of subsidies (Table 3.3). These have been provided by a multiplicity of agencies, among others MAJUIKAN, BPM, the Fisheries Division of the Ministry of Agriculture and FAMA, resulting in duplication and inter-agency competition, but with little visible impact. Inexperienced officers from these agencies or the cooperatives they sponsored, have attempted to play the role of trainers or mentors to the traditional fishermen in a futile attempt at converting them from artisanal to commercial, mechanised entrpreneurs. This was attempted by means of various subsidy programmes that provided new, top-of-the-line equipment, including boats, motors and nets, often free, save for political considerations. This paternalistic and amateurish approach ended in frustration and cynicism along with large amounts of wasted public resources.[24]

The main shortcoming of the Malaysian fishery policy stems from the presumption that in the long-run it is an economically viable activity. Hence subsidies, marketing and other bureaucratic services, specifically designed for artisanal fishermen on the East Coast, have been provided with no serious consideration of an alternative strategy of encouraging the transfer of excess labour from a declining industry to more productive ones. In recent years, this policy conflict has been considerably sharpened by the discovery of oil and gas off the shore of Trengganu. As this event will dramatically and inevitably transform the local economy by inflating the wage, price and cost structures, it is bound to accelerate the rate of decline in Malay artisanal fishing. Therefore, far from subsidising traditional fishing, the required future policy intervention lies in facilitating the transfer of labour to more productive employment in other activities. A major constraint in such a strategy lies in the level of investment in *local* human resource development to increase the supply of technical and vocational skills as a means of raising the productivity and income-earning capacity of local labour. Unfortunately, however, this is not what the Malaysian authorities are doing. In fact, they are increasingly relying on imported, expatriate manpower which tends to minimise local employment and income creation.

Tax Discrimination against Rubber Smallholders

One of the oldest and most important forms of regressive fiscal policy in Malaysia (and previously in British Malaya) is tax discrimination against rubber smallholders. Bauer and other economic historians have amply documented the colonial bias against rubber smallholders.[25] Remarkably, the smallholders are still subject to the same regressive taxes. They are taxed at the same rate as the estates. There are three such taxes: (a) the export duty — 22.125 cents/kg, (b) the research cess — 3.85 cents/kg and (c) the replanting cess — 4.5 cents/kg.[26]

These taxes are collected and distributed by different agencies, independently of the Ministry of Finance. The export duty is collected by the Malaysian Rubber Exchange and Licensing Board, while the research and replanting cesses are collected by the Malaysian Rubber Research and Development Board. These revenues finance the research activities of the Rubber Research Institute of Malaysia and the replanting scheme of RISDA.

The tax burden of these duties and cesses, expressed as a proportion of the income of households and estates, is regressive. In fact, effective tax discrimination is considerably higher than the nominal tax rates, since, for example, most of the benefits of the research cess accrue primarily to the estates which have the capacity to utilise the research findings because of their larger scale of operations. Similarly, the replanting subsidy is administered in a manner benefiting estates. Whereas estates receive a full refund of their paid-out replanting cess, the smallholders are entitled to a grant only after they actually replant and, even then, they are repaid in yearly instalments.

The amount of grant offered depends on the size of the holding and type of tree replanted. For holdings under ten acres the grant (as revised in 1980) is $2,200 per acre if replanted with rubber and $1,800 if replanted with another crop. If the holding exceeds ten acres, these figures are $1,500 and $1,200 respectively.

Participation in RISDA's replanting scheme has been less than expected. According to a comprehensive survey in 1977,[27] there were a total of 490,460 registered rubber smallholders in Peninsular Malaysia. Of these, 124,590 had relatively new trees as a result of participation in other agency programmes — such as those of FELDA and FELCRA — or own-account replanting. Of the remaining 365,870, no less than 107,636 or 29.4 per cent with old trees and quite eligible for grant, did not participate in RISDA's scheme. Over 80 per cent of the non-participants were Malays and about half had holdings of less than two hectares (Table 3.4).

Why is the non-participation rate in RISDA's replanting scheme so high, especially among the Malays who are the focal target group? While there are several cultural and social factors involved, the small uneconomic size of their holdings is of fundamental importance since it is the key determinant of the ultimate profitability of replanting. How can a poor rubber smallholding family be expected to bear the cost and risk of forgone income associated with replanting for as long as six years? Unlike estates or larger producers, the smallholder is unable to diversify his crops and

Table 3.4: Distribution of Non-Participants in RISDA's Replanting
Scheme, by size of Holdings and Race, 1977

Size of Holdings (hectares)	Bumiputera No.	%	Chinese No.	%	Others No.	%	Total No.	%
0.01 – 1.99	46,089	51.1	3,276	21.6	1,235	53.4	50,600	47.0
2.00 – 3.99	33,864	37.6	7,277	48.0	881	38.1	42,022	39.0
>4.00	10,203	11.3	4,616	30.4	195	8.4	15,014	14.0
Total	90,156	100.0	15,169	100.0	2,311	100.0	107,636	100.0
%	83.8		14.1		2.1		100.0	

Source: RISDA (Draft Final Report, 1982), Table 4.11, p. 151

inter-space replanting in order to minimise forgone income to acceptable levels of risk. In 1981 RISDA introduced a new SEPENTAS scheme specifically for this category of families. Under this scheme, families with less than two hectares of rubber are provided with an interest-free loan of $100 per month, and $60 per month if they own between two and four hectares.[28] These repayable loans can last for up to six years until rubber trees mature. No evidence is available on the effectiveness of this new scheme, but it is surprising that the Malaysian authorities expect *loans* to be a more attractive inducement to the poorest of the poor smallholders when grants for families with larger holdings suffer from serious problems of non-participation.

The rubber price policy is also characterised by an indifference to the economic welfare of the smallholders. On the one hand, Malaysia has actively supported the *international* stabilisation of natural rubber prices through buffer stock management by the International Natural Rubber Organisation (INRO), out of concern for stabilising the country's foreign exchange earnings. Indeed, INRO has been quite successful in this role, thanks, in significant measure, to supportive market interventions by Malaysia.[29] On the other hand, however, the Malaysian government has shown little interest in a *domestic* income stabilisation scheme to protect rubber producers, especially the smallholders, whose incomes remain linked to severe price fluctuations in international commodity markets. Despite repeated demonstrations by small-scale producers even after the 1974 Baling riots,[30] the Malaysian government sought international action rather than establishing a domestic income stabilisation scheme. Such a scheme could be financed in a manner comparable to, for example, the research or the replanting funds.

Rice Policy: Output Maximisation or Poverty Redressal?

The Malaysian government's rice policy was designed to maximise output first and foremost in conformity with the objective of national self-sufficiency. The policymakers assumed that this objective could be achieved within the existing structure of land ownership and therefore new farm technologies were introduced without any attempt at land reform.

The strategy of maximising rice output began in earnest soon after Merdeka, gaining momentum in the mid-1960s with considerable financial support from the World Bank. During the period of the First Malaysia Plan, 1966–70, a total of $328.5 million public expenditure was invested in drainage and irrigation works at the giant Muda and Kemubu schemes.[31] At the same time, the 'Green Revolution' technology was introduced in the form of high-yielding seeds, fertilisers and mechanised farming. As a result, traditional methods of rice farming were revolutionised. There was a rapid decline in wet-season cultivation and an expansion of dry-season cultivation as irrigation facilities and new technological inputs led

Table 3.5: Padi Area, Yield and Production in Major IADP Schemes, 1970–1981

Scheme and Year	Area harvested (hec.)			Yield (Ton/hec.)		Total production
	Dry season	Wet season	Total	Dry season	Wet season	
1. MADA						
1970	30,567	95,859	126,426	3.8	3.6	461,247
1981	90,208	93,242	183,450	3.7	4.0	706,738
% Change	195.1	−2.7	45.1	−2.6	11.1	53.2
2. KADA I						
1970	1,209	18,181	19,390	2.5	2.5	48,474
1981	12,849	11,495	24,344	3.6	3.7	88,802
% Change	962.8	−36.8	25.5	44.0	48.0	83.2
3. KADA II						
1970	8,837	29,794	38,631	2.7	2.4	95,366
1981	18,836	14,385	33,221	3.4	3.6	115,828
% Change	113.1	−51.7	−14.0	25.9	50.0	21.5
4. Besut						
1970	1,010	5,260	6,270	1.9	1.6	10,160
1981	3,035	4,250	7,285	3.5	3.5	23,194
% Change	200.5	−19.2	16.2	84.2	118.8	128.3

Source: Sukor Kasim, *et al., Study of Strategy*, Vol. II, Appendix Tables 2.2(a), 2.2(b), 2.2(c) and 2.2(e).

to double-cropping and commercialised farming (Table 3.5). By the end of 1970, about 620,000 acres or 65.7 per cent of the 943,000 acres of rice lands had been provided with irrigation facilities and about 286,000 acres or 46 per cent of the irrigated acreage had been placed under double-cropping.[32]

Output Growth. These investments and technological inputs did, indeed, achieve impressive gains in terms of production and yield rates. In MADA, total rice production increased by 53.2 per cent during 1970–81 and yields in the wet season rose by 11.1 per cent but declined by 2.6 per cent in dry-season cultivation. In KADA I, the production gain over the same period was 83.2 per cent and yield rates improved by 44 per cent and 48 per cent in dry and wet seasons respectively. In KADA II the gains in production were less. In Besut, production rose by 128.3 per cent in wet season (Table 3.5). Overall, the area under rice cultivation increased by 68,000 hectares during 1970–80, while the yield rate per hectare rose from 1,055 gantangs to 1,260 gantangs. Total rice production registered a 33 per cent increase going from 1.434 million tons in 1970 to 1.913 million tons in 1980.[33]

Trends in Average Incomes. There were also significant increases in the average real incomes of households in areas of major padi schemes.[34] In the Muda scheme in Perlis and Kedah owner-operator households averaged $2,023 in 1979 (in 1967 prices) compared to $1,379 in 1966, a gain of 47 per cent. In the KADA scheme in Kelantan average real household income rose from $647 in 1968 to $1,926 (in 1967 prices), almost a threefold increase. In Besut, the income gain was less, from $1,001 in 1971 to $1,288 in 1978. However, in all these schemes a significant proportion of income was earned from off-farm employment, indicating that padi investments and technological inputs were less productive than average income trends would at first suggest. Moreover, these averages are subject to substantial variations and fail to reflect the maldistribution of income and wealth among padi farmers which actually became worse.

Another factor contributing to higher average incomes among padi farmers was the effect of rice subsidies introduced under the Fourth Malaysia Plan.[35] While these positively affected average household incomes, the benefits were distributed in favour of the larger and wealthier farmers who are more politically influential.

As a result, they contributed to intra-community inequality of income and asset distribution.

Indirect Effects. Local community income distribution was also worsened by the indirect, downstream effects of investments in large-scale rice irrigation projects. Their benefits accrued primarily to non-farm households engaged in rice milling and non-tradeables. According to an evaluation of the Muda irrigation project, every additional dollar of value added in padi production, generated by the project at maturity, resulted in about 75 cents of value added elsewhere in the Malaysian economy by the indirect effects of the project. Each dollar of downstream value added probably supported over a dollar of additional investment in plant and equipment in the project area.[36]

The Move to Self-sufficiency. In 1973 there was a crisis in Malaysian rice imports as a result of Thailand's ban on rice export to prevent a threatened domestic shortage. As a result, the Malaysian government adopted a policy target of 100% self-sufficiency. This gave additional impetus to infrastructural investments and modernisation efforts in the rice sector thereafter. Under the Third Malaysia Plan of 1976–80, the revised allocation for drainage and irrigation works was increased to $828.86 million, more than double that of the Second Malaysia Plan of 1971–75 (Table 2.1). By 1980 the level of self-sufficiency had been raised to 92 per cent compared to 78 per cent in 1970.[37] But Malaysia is a comparatively high-cost rice producer. The 2,850 kg per hectare achieved in the MADA scheme — the most efficient in the country — is significantly below Japan (5,330 kg/hec.), Korea (4,918 kg/hec.) or Australia (5,330 kg/hec.).[38] The social costs of subsidising the policy of rice self-sufficiency have been high and regressive.

The Pricing and Regulation of Rice

The central feature of the regulatory system in the rice sector is the Guaranteed Minimum Price (GMP), originally introduced by the colonial authorities in 1946 to increase post-war production. It was a policy with a strong 'urban bias' intended to feed urban populations, and this bias has, of course, remained in force.

In the early 1960s, following Independence, when the cooperative movement was particularly favoured, GMP was linked to the officially-sanctioned 'comprehensive co-operative marketing and credit system'.[39] The cooperatives were granted monopsony powers on padi purchase at the expense of private traders in several states. Nevertheless, this attempt to introduce cooperatives into the rice and padi sector failed within a few years, because the cooperatives became increasingly uncompetitive. They began to regard the GMP as a fixed 'fair' price, rather than a minimum price as it was originally intended to be. There were also delays in payments and other causes of dissatisfaction among farmers who, as a result, increasingly preferred doing business with private merchants and dealers.

In 1966 the government, acting on the undiminished assumption that the private rice and padi market was too imperfect and exploitative to be left unregulated, established a new Federal Agricultural Marketing Authority (FAMA). FAMA's task was to promote the efficient and effective marketing of agricultural products by reinforcing the limited bargaining power of producers, providing market information, regulating grades and standards and eliminating middlemen monopsony, cartels and price-fixing arrangements.[40] During 1966–68, FAMA undertook some fact-gathering surveys of padi marketing and this helped in deciding to set up a new National Padi and Rice Marketing Board (LPN). It was empowered to control rice prices in Malaysia through a variety of measures including buffer stockpiling, licensing of import quotas and compulsory sales by millers and wholesalers.[41]

LPN became operational at the beginning of 1972. For its buffer stock management, LPN purchases rice through two channels; by direct purchases from farmers at the prevailing GMP and from millers at the equivalent of GMP for milled rice. For this second channel, LPN undertakes to purchase good, dry padi delivered at the mill door. 'Good padi' is specified as 'padi fully matured, of not more than 13 per cent moisture content, free of dirt, empty grains, husk, straw and other foreign matter'.[42] A deduction is made if the moisture content exceeds 13 per cent. The GMP was $16 per picul until 1979 when it was raised to $28–32 and further increased to $36–40 in 1980.[43]

Three of the main problems with the LPN price support scheme are: (a) it misallocates resources by encouraging the production of high-cost, low-quality domestic rice, (b) its redistributive effects are significantly regressive and (c) its subsidy management is fraught with waste and inefficiency.

Resource Misallocation Effect. In line with the objective of rice self-sufficiency, LPN controls imports through quota licensing. Recipients of these licences are required to purchase local rice from LPN's accumulated stocks, in a ratio that is determined as a policy instrument.[44] In this way, low-quality, high-cost local rice is marketed by traders to domestic consumers in conjunction with the better-quality imported rice and sold at variable prices. Traders usually sell local rice at a loss but they more than recover their losses from the profitable sale of imported rice.

The effect of this subsidy system on resource allocation is that it blocks land, labour and other productive resources in high-cost padi production which, under a more competitive regime, would be too uneconomic and the resources thus would be obliged to move into alternative, more remunerative, uses. More specifically, it can be argued that the subsidy system perpetuates poverty among padi farmers by encouraging under-employment and by slowing the rate of labour transfer into off-farm income and employment opportunities.

Policy alternatives to domestic rice and padi cultivation need to be based on the premise that its long-term viability is doubtful not only on the basis of relative costs but also in view of the fact that, with increasing incomes, the Malaysian diet will change in favour of alternative food items. Thus, diversification rather than self-sufficiency offers a more rational approach to resource allocation.

One important aspect of rural development which has been neglected in policies of resource allocation is small-scale industries. Statistical data regarding small-scale industries in Malaysia, especially in rural areas, is virtually non-existent. Judging from the growth of off-farm income and employment opportunities it is evident that there has been significant expansion of small-scale rural industries, despite the lack of any supportive policies. The potential for growth of such industries is far from being exhausted. It is clearly one aspect of rural development which deserves greater priority in order to promote more efficient alternative resource allocation.

Regressive Redistributive Effects. The producer subsidy based on the GMP is financed indirectly by rice consumers in general and by the lower-income households in particular for whom the higher-quality imported rice is too costly. In fact, it has been estimated that the price of low-quality local rice was 19 per cent higher than what it would have been in the event of free trade rice prices.[45] This burden is now significantly greater as a result of higher subsidy levels. Since the consumption of local rice is inversely related to income, it is evident that the burden of the producer subsidy falls heavily on the poorer households. Thus, it is not unreasonable to argue that the overall effect of the LPN subsidy system is to retain poor padi farmers in marginal production, the cost of doing so being borne by all consumers, particularly the low-income families.

Subsidy Mismanagement. Furthermore, the LPN's administration of the subsidy programme is so fraught with abuses and mismanagement that it tends to benefit more the middlemen — millers and traders as well as the officials themselves — than the producers. One method by which middlemen in rice trading benefit is through the licensing system which favours the politically well-connected. The abuses of the early 'agency system' have already been noted.[46] Under the 'coupon system', introduced in 1980, farmers were supposed to get $10 coupons for each sack of 60 kg of rice they sold to the LPN. The number of coupons would be determined on the basis of bills of sale issued by the millers. In fact, many millers, sometimes with the active collaboration of farmers, were in the habit of overstating the amount of padi on their bills of sale as a means of extra profit-making. In some cases, these fraudulent practices involved LPN officials.[47]

The same form of mismanagement occurs in the fertiliser subsidy programmes. In the case of padi cultivation, fertilisers are sold at subsidised prices to farmers through the FOs and, in theory, poor farmers are entitled to grants and low-interest loans from the BPM. However, these benefits have effectively been monopolised by the wealthy and influential, often working through organised syndicates.[48] For example, in February 1982, the Chairman of the BPM reported that 38 per cent of the 261 persons obtaining interest-free loans and 57 per cent of those who borrowed at 2 per cent interest rates were not 'genuine' full-time or poor farmers.[49] On the other hand, 30 per cent of the poor farming households in the Muda scheme are reported to be in perpetual debt, not for consumption credits as under the *padi kunca* system, but for credit purchases of fertilisers. In fact, these credits have actually increased dramatically, rising from $417 per family in 1966 to $2,772 in 1978/79.[50]

Conclusion. The result emerging from the above review is that large-scale government intervention with price supports, fertiliser subsidies, grants and credits as well as infrastructural investments have failed to cure mass poverty among padi farmers. In fact, technology and commercialised farming led to large-scale displacement of tenants and dispossession of small farmers.[51] Greater impoverishment was ameliorated, to a degree, by expanding off-farm income opportunities. The paradox is that intervention was justified in terms of elimination of perceived market imperfections and unfair trade practices in the private sector. Empirical evidence suggests that this was an exaggerated presumption.[52] Nevertheless, it has resulted in the proliferation of a top-heavy bureaucracy which has practically taken over, or supplemented, the functions of middlemen and, in the process, has significantly increased the social costs of marketing, processing and related transactions.

One of the most recent new policy announcements is the National Agricultural Policy (NAP)[53] intended to promote farm efficiency through greater emphasis on commercialisation. As far as padi cultivation is concerned, NAP makes some vague references to cooperative farming. Given the disappointing history of this approach in the past, it is unlikely to prove successful in future. On the other hand, increased farm commercialisation, without complementary policies to absorb released labour in alternative productive employment, is (as demonstrated by past experience) bound to multiply poverty.

The FELDA Model of Land Development: a 'Modernising Agent' or Plantation Company?

We now examine the show-piece of the Malaysian agricultural and rural development strategy, from the perspective of its impact on rural poverty: the FELDA model of land development and settlement. FELDA settlers, typically Malay padi farmers and rubber tappers, are generally regarded as the government's *anak emas* — favourite children — because they are considered the lucky ones selected to escape poverty.

In terms of public expenditure, allocations for the FELDA model have consistently been by far the largest component of the agricultural and rural development budget, accounting for around half the total (Table 2.1). By the end of 1981, FELDA itself had developed 564,910 hectares of jungle land into plantations, and

Table 3.6: FELDA Land Development and Settlement up to the End of 1981

	No. of schemes	Area (hec.)	Settler Families
Oil palm	177	335,741	40,256
Rubber	117	178,322	29,685
Cocoa	11	15,059	182
Sugar cane	2	5,118	440
Coffee	1	529	—
Town/Village	—	30,141	—
Total	308	564,910	70,563

Source: FELDA: Annual Report, 1981

had settled a total of 70,563 families, typically with an 8–10 acre holding or equivalent revenue share (Table 3.6).

FELDA has a split personality, which accounts both for its success and failure. On the one hand, it is a large plantation company, relying upon the time-tested, colonial techniques of estate management, including the use of exploited labour in a profitable business. On the other hand, it is a 'modernising agency'[54] expected to transform rural poverty into mass prosperity for the *rakyat*. These two objectives are inherently conflicting and, in recent years, FELDA's split-personality complex has become more acute as the Authority has tended to divert increasing surpluses to growth and diversification at the expense of its objectives of poverty amelioration.

Land Development as an Anti-poverty Policy Instrument

As an instrument of anti-poverty policy, the FELDA model has been based on the key assumption that mass prosperity for the *rakyat* can be created in the plantation sector. In turn this key assumption emerged from the 'demonstration effect' of the fabulous profits realised by European planters and investors dating back to the rubber boom of the early twentieth century.[55] The magical attraction persisted in the minds of the peasants, despite repeated attempts by colonial authorities to contain it, giving rise to the so-called 'land hunger' phenomenon. At the time of Independence in 1957 there were at least 100,000 applicants anxious for a stake in the land development and settlement for which FELDA was created in the preceding year.[56]

As a plantation company, FELDA strives to achieve economies of scale through large-scale land schemes, concentrating on rubber and oil palm produced for export markets. As an 'integrated' land settlement project, each FELDA scheme is packaged as a new, self-sufficient community, complete with roads, water, dwellings, schools, health clinics, irrigation and drainage works, transportation, and marketing and processing facilities. Originally, the typical FELDA scheme was relatively small, ranging between 4000–5000 acres accommodating 400 settler families, but in the late 1960s, giant-sized projects — e.g. the Jengka Triangle, Johore Tenggara, and Pahang Tenggara — were undertaken covering millions of acres and thousands of settler families.[57]

At the outset, FELDA was conceived as no more than a federal funding agency, supplying finance to state governments which would actually implement land settlement and development projects. There was no intention for FELDA to be actively involved in the implementation since, under the Malaysian constitution, land matters are exclusively the prerogative of the states and their Sultans. Subsequently, however, implementation delays and difficulties were encountered[58] and FELDA gradually began to assume an increasingly direct and active role as an implementing and central management agency. By 1981 it had become one of the largest plantation companies not only in Malaysia but in the world. Its annual budget allocation for 1981 was $538 million, derived from both the Malaysian government and external sources, principally the World Bank and Arab banking interests. Its cumulative drawings from the government at the end of 1981 stood at $3.0 billion.[59]

FELDA relies on private land contractors for the establishment of the first phase of its schemes. Land clearing, planting and infrastructural works are all contracted to private firms who often subcontract portions of the work to smaller contractors. The development costs are fully privatised in that they are ultimately recovered from the settlers during the income-generating phase of the scheme. The settlers are brought into the scheme when the production phase is to start, four years after planting in the case of oil palm and six in the case of rubber. Each settler family is provided with a standard house, a garden plot for growing vegetables and fruit, and an 8–10 acre holding, for which the settler can expect to get a title in 15 years' time. The title, to be issued by the state in which the scheme is located, can only be obtained after full repayment of the development costs plus any accumulated credit arrears. The development costs, together with a long list of other deductions from gross income, are withheld by FELDA prior to computing the settler's net income. Once the scheme enters its productive, revenue-generating phase, lasting about 20−25 years, the settler's income is derived from the proceeds of the main crop, sold through FELDA which receives the revenue and then pays the settler a monthly net income. Since settlers' incomes are derived from primary export crops, they can, and do, experience sharp monthly swings, caused by sudden fluctuations in the price of rubber and oil palm. FELDA has not developed an income stabilisation scheme for its settlers, although there are funds for research and replanting. It has introduced a credit system for making fully recoverable advances if and when net monthly income drops below $350 per month in the case of oil palm, and $250 per month in the case of rubber plantations.[60]

Weaknesses of the FELDA Model

Some of the main weaknesses of the FELDA model relate to: (a) settler selection and development, (b) titles and private property, and (c) cost, ecology and structural constraints. The fundamental problem, which has been largely ignored in the past, concerns the use of the surplus generated by FELDA as a plantation company. These four problems will now be discussed.

Settler Selection and Development. FELDA settlers are actually selected by politicians and high-level officials, primarily on political criteria. Over 95 per cent of the settlers are Malay, with a strong preference given to padi farmers, rubber tappers, fishermen and ex-servicemen. The typical settler is male, about 30 years old, married with an expanding family and has little relevant experience in estate management in a cooperative environment. As a result, numerous problems have been encountered in field maintenance and production operations. For example, on rubber schemes, there is overtapping when high prices prevail. There are always illegal sales of latex and scrap to private dealers in order to avoid FELDA deductions or to earn quick income. The quality of tree management varies significantly from one holding to the next, depending on the entrepreneurial motivations of the settlers, their ability to use fertilisers effectively, to weed and maintain fields properly, to tap and harvest according to weather conditions, tree biology and other technical requirements. Thus, in one holding, managed by a poorly motivated and careless settler, the trees may acquire various kinds of disease, threatening other holdings and creating neighbourhood conflicts and endangering the economic viability of the entire scheme.

Titles and Private Property. In view of these problems, FELDA has, in recent years, begun to replace the traditional 'individual holding' system with the 'block system' of settler ownership. The latter is a more corporatist than a private ownership approach to estate management. Under the block system, settlers are no longer issued titles to individual holdings. Instead they are assured of an income share equivalent to the 8–10 acres holding. Management of the scheme is then organised on a collective basis with a common, scheme-wide maintenance and production operation. While the block system tends to minimise operational problems, it runs counter to the dominant concept of private ownership among the Malays and it is likely to make the settlers think of themselves as merely estate workers in conflict with FELDA.[61] Thus, on a number of schemes, FELDA has had difficulty in ensuring adequate labour supply from settlers and has been obliged to rely on labour contractors, some of whom have practised near-slavery and other forms of exploitation.[62]

Another serious problem regarding titles has been the long delays in the granting of them by the relevant state authorities. In the vast majority of cases these delays stem from unpaid loans and arrears, since the pre-condition for entitlement is that all settlers' accounts must be fully paid. However, under the existing system of settler compensation, this is typically impossible, and settlers are obliged to accumulate large amounts of credit and borrowings from FELDA which effectively prevent entitlement.

Cost, Ecology and Structural Constraints. The FELDA model is a high-cost method of attempting to reduce rural poverty. The average cost per settler (in 1980 prices) is about $30,000.[63] At this rate, it would require $13.3 billion to settle the 443,700 poor households (Table 2.3) on FELDA schemes — an amount which is 60 per cent higher than the total Fourth Malaysia Plan allocation for agriculture and rural development. Cost, however, is neither the only nor the most important constraint. There are significant administrative and operational difficulties. At the current rate of resettlement of about 5,000 settlers annually, it would take almost 90 years to settle the 443,700 rural poor households. While there may be sufficient reserves of undeveloped jungle land suitable for development and settlement in Malaysia, much of this land is in East Malaysia. In Peninsular Malaysia, where most rural poverty is concentrated, serious legal and ecological constraints have been encountered.

In addition, there are major problems resulting from the structure and pattern of the plantation system. In effect, the fixed land-labour ratio contains a built-in underemployment trap stemming from the population growth on the FELDA schemes. While the ratio of 8–10 acres per settler may be adequate for the first generation of households, it is unlikely to be so for subsequent generations. Already, the children of the original settlers, referred to as 'FELDA children',[64] are faced with limited income and employment opportunities and are forced into underemployment or migration.

One of the most serious structural problems with the FELDA model is that of income instability. The economic welfare of the settlers is dependent on price fluctuations in the world commodity markets, and these are reinforced by variations in output resulting from seasonal and botanical factors. As we have already discussed above,[65] there is no domestic income stabilisation scheme to protect settlers' incomes from commodity price cycles and, as a result, these incomes can range from $400 to $1,500 a month several times during the course of one year.

Analysis of Settler Incomes on Two FELDA Schemes

In order to examine settler incomes in detail, we shall now isolate two specific schemes previously evaluated.[66] These two schemes are: Bukit Rokan Utara, Phase I (rubber), and Pasoh 4, Phase I (oil palm). In Table 3.7, average settler incomes per month, computed and verified by FELDA head office, are presented. Gross income (col. 2) refers to income before deductions (col. 4). These deductions, specified at the bottom of Table 3.7, are treated by FELDA as *fixed costs* invariant with respect to fluctuating prices. Thus, the settler's income is a *residual* which fluctuates fully with commodity prices. Net income (col. 3) is what the settler actually receives, net of all of deductions, but inclusive of a cash supplement given as repayable credits, as explained below. These are loans and accumulate as arrears (col. 5).

Judging from gross and net income figures, the economic position of FELDA settlers is extremely impressive, bearing in mind pre-settlement average incomes. In the rubber scheme under

Table 3.7: Average Monthly Settlers' Income and Arrears in 2 FELDA Schemes, 1980–1983 (All figures in $)

1	2	3	4	5	6
Year	Gross (G)	Supplemented net cash (NC)	Deductions (d)[a]	Arrears[b]	True net income[c]
Bukit Rokan Utara Ph. 1 (Rubber)					
1980	784.27	548.31	699.86	463.90	84.41
1981	992.08	756.70	853.83	618.45	138.25
1982	1,061.29	769.97	965.07	673.75	96.22
1983[d]	1,346.91	1,033.47	903.86	590.42	443.05
					$\overline{X}$ = 190.48
Pasoh 4, Ph. 1 (oil palm)					
1980	790.22	499.15	515.60	224.53	274.62
1981	942.55	543.05	504.84	105.34	437.71
1982	1,053.64	683.82	584.31	214.49	469.33
1983[d]	768.98	488.04	577.59	296.65	191.39
					$\overline{X}$ = 343.26

Notes: a. Including FELDA and Personal deductions
       b. Arrears = G – d – NC
       c. True net income (G – d) = Net cash – Arrears
       d. Jan–Oct
       $\overline{X}$ = average for 1980–83
Source: Settlers Income Division, FELDA

review, the average monthly net income rose from about $500 in 1980 to over $1,000 in 1983. If we use a rural poverty level of an annual income of $3,000 as the typical pre-settlement income, it would appear that these settlers are well out of poverty, realising up to four times the poverty-level income.

In fact, this is quite misleading as can be seen from the amount of accumulated arrears (col. 5) and the true net income (col. 6). This last amount is the take-home pay without the credit supplement. In the case of Bukit Rokan Utara it represents only 16.7 per cent of gross income during 1980–83. In the case of Pasoh 4 it is 37.6 per cent. For settlers on the Bukit Rokan Utara scheme, the annual average take-home pay over 1980–83 works out to $2,280, which is well below the poverty-level income of $3,000. In the case of Pasoh 4, this average is significantly higher at $4,110, but nowhere near the level suggested by gross and net income figures.

There are two key factors in the analysis of settler incomes above. First, the FELDA policy of fixed deductions effectively passes the burden of instability in commodity prices fully on to the shoulders of settlers. Secondly, the loan/credit policy actually promotes settler indebtedness. The motivation behind this last policy is to avoid extreme fluctuations in settler incomes. Accordingly, the credit system of supplementing monthly take-home pay, erroneously called a 'guaranteed income', has been designed so that settlers on rubber estates are assured of a minimum monthly cash payment of $250, while those on oil palm schemes are similarly assured of $350. These credits take the form of repayable cash loans or credit purchases at FELDA shops.

As can be seen from Table 3.7, these arrears can be extremely high. On the Bukit Rokan Utara scheme (not necessarily a typical one), during the four years 1980–83, they amounted to $28,158 per settler, while on the Pasoh 4 scheme they were $10,092 per settler. The crucial fact is that these credit supplements, like loan repayments, must be fully discharged before settlers can qualify for titles. The FELDA policy is to require 15 years for these repayments against a scheme's productive life of 20–25 years. The effect of credit arrears is to postpone the prospect of entitlement well beyond the 15-year period. In fact, the repayment policy would appear to rule out entitlement during the productive life of the schemes, except in the case of exceptionally profitable schemes.

Problems of credit arrears are common on FELDA schemes, although the magnitude of indebtedness may vary significantly from one scheme to the next. However, the severity of the problem can be gauged from the fact that out of a total of more than 300 schemes developed by FELDA to the end of 1983, only six schemes had been able to qualify for entitlement.[67]

The position of settlers on schemes developed by a multitude of other agencies is no better — more than likely it is worse. Therefore, it is hardly surprising that in a recent survey of FELDA and KEJORA (Johore Tenggara Land Development Authority), it was found that more than 86 per cent of settlers stated that they did not want their children to remain on the schemes[68] — a strong indicator of settler dissatisfaction. Another indication of such dissatisfaction is the recurring series of demonstrations and protests against working and living conditions on land schemes.[69] In one recent incident, the Minister of Land and Regional Development, together with 20 officers, was locked in a room for seven and a half hours by angry settlers. Police had to be brought in to disperse the mob and release the Minister.[70]

*FELDA Investments: The Emergence of a Diversified
Conglomerate*

Despite settler indebtedness and dissatisfaction, FELDA is a
profitable enterprise. In 1981 its total revenue from production was
$702.2 million which was 23.4 per cent higher than in the previous
year.[71] Of this revenue, $52.4 million, 7.5 per cent, represented loan
repayments to the federal government and to external lenders such
as the World Bank and various Arab interests. Land rent charges
payable to state governments accounted for $9.1 million or 1.3 per
cent. Up to half the production revenue represented settlers'
incomes. The balance, up to 40 per cent, in the form of surplus
revenue, was diverted into reserve funds, in part to finance future
replanting.

   Most of the net balance is utilised to finance corporate expansion
and diversification of the company. Some of this is justifiable on
the usual criteria of backward and forward linkage since it involves
the marketing and processing of main crops. Thus, in recent years,
FELDA has entered into several joint ventures with multinational
corporations (e.g. Nestlé of Switzerland, Mitsui and Asahi of
Japan and Vandermoortele of Holland). It has also acquired a
major interest in Boustead Holding Bhd., a previously British-
owned plantation company in Malaysia, and has invested in a large
number of other companies, including Batu Kawan, Malayan
Banking, Highlands & Lowlands and KL Kepong.[72]

   However, priority for growth and diversification appears to be
pursued at the expense of the economic welfare of the settlers. They
are squeezed not only by the credit system discussed above but also
by a policy of 'forced savings' actively promoted by the management in their pursuit of savings mobilisation over current consumption. The FELDA technique of utilising forced savings and profits
to generate surplus for corporate growth and diversification is a
direct consequence of the NEP's trusteeship system. It provides a
major explanation for the failure of rural development strategies
under the trusteeship to solve the problem of poverty. Recently,
FELDA has expressed a desire to join the current fashion in
Malaysia of becoming 'privatised',[73] which may signal the end of
any pretence that FELDA is playing any 'modernising' or anti-
poverty role.

Notes

1. Ungku Abdul Aziz, 'Poverty and Rural Development', *Kajian Ekonomi Malaysia*, vol. I, no. 1, June 1964, pp. 70–105.
2. *Kunca* is a volume measure of 160 gantangs of rice. The credit system worked as follows: the merchants and dealers would provide the padi farmer credit for both consumption and production purposes against repayment in padi at harvest time in terms of *kunca*. Often these credit arrangements were unwritten obligations and carried exorbitant rates of interest resulting in perpetual indebtedness for the farmer. For a brief account, see J. J. Puthucheary, *Ownership and Control in the Malayan Economy*, pp. 8–10. Also, see Mokhzani bin Abdul Rahim and Khoo Siew Min, eds, *Some Case Studies on Poverty in Malaysia*, Persatuan Ekonomi Malaysia, Kuala Lumpur, 1977. For a more analytical treatment, see Clifton R. Wharton, Jr., 'Marketing, Merchandising and Moneylending: A Note on Middleman Monopsony in Malaya', *Malayan Economic Review*, vol. VII, no. 2, October 1962, pp. 24–44.
   Rural indebtedness, however, is a complex phenomenon, and the effect of middlemen exploitation may easily be exaggerated. Thus evidence from field surveys does not confirm the existence of excessive price spreads. See, for example, John Purcal, *Rice Economy: A Case Study of Four Villages in West Malaysia*, University of Malaya Press, Kuala Lumpur, 1971, esp. pp. 121–4; and more recently, Kenzo Horii, *Rice Economy and Land Tenure in Malaysia*, Institute of Developing Economies, Tokyo, 1981, esp. pp. 131–7.
3. S. C. Lim, *A Study of the Marketing of Smallholders' Rubber at the First Trade Level in Selangor*, RRIM, Economic and Planning Division, Kuala Lumpur, 1968; S. T. Cheam, *A Study of the Marketing of Smallholders' Lower Grade Rubber*, RRIM, Economic and Planning Division, Kuala Lumpur, 1971; C. Barlow, *The Natural Rubber Industry, Its Development, Technology and Economy in Malaysia*, Oxford University Press, Kuala Lumpur, 1978, pp. 316–20.
4. Yap Chang Ling, 'Poverty in the Fishing Industry: An Analysis of the Profit Sharing Systems in the Dindings' in Mokhzani and Khoo, *Some Case Studies*, pp. 55–70.
5. Chandra Muzaffar, *Protector?*; Bruce Gale, *Politics and Public Enterprise in Malaysia*.
6. Gayl D. Ness, *Bureaucracy and Rural Development in Malaysia,* University of California Press, Berkeley, 1967.
7. John Slimming, *Malaysia: Death of a Democracy*, John Murray, London, 1969.
8. See the *Second Malaysia Plan, 1971–75* which set out the original quantitative targets of the Overall Perspective Plan (OPP) during 1970–90. The 'two prongs' of the NEP were first stated in the *Third Malaysia Plan, 1976–80*, para. 27, p. 7.
9. For a brief survey of the various marketing schemes, see R. W. A. Vokes, 'Reforming Food Grain Markets: Some Lessons From Malaysia's Experience in Padi Marketing', *Kajian Ekonomi Malaysia*, vol. 16, nos. 1 and 2, June–December, 1979, pp. 202–22.
10. See pp. 59–61.
11. For a more detailed account of the group processing centres, see George Cho, 'The Location of Development Centres for Rubber Smallholders in Peninsular Malaysia' in *Issues in Malaysian Development* edited by James C. Jackson and Martin Rudner, Heinemann, Kuala Lumpur, 1980, pp. 101–12.
12. See pp. 54–5.
13. For a recent evaluation of IADPs, see Sukor Kasim, *et al., Study of Strategy, Impact and Future Development of Integrated Agricultural Development Projects* (2 volumes), Centre for Policy Research, Universiti Sains Malaysia, Penang, March 1983.

14. For a historical account of FELDA, see Shamsul Bahrin, P. D. A. Perera and Lim Heng Kow, *FELDA — 21 Years of Land Development*, University of Malaya, Kuala Lumpur, 1977; C. MacAndrews, *Mobility and Modernization: The Federal Land Development Authority and Its Role in Modernizing the Rural Malays*, Gadjah Mada University Press, Yogjakarta, 1977.

15. See Ch. 5, pp. 76–9.

16. Vokes, 'Reforming Food Grain Markets', pp. 217–18.

17. Cho, 'Location of Development Centres', p. 126.

18. Ozay Mehmet, 'Evaluating Alternative Land Schemes in Malaysia: FELDA and FELCRA', *Contemporary Southeast Asia*, vol. 3, no. 4, 1982, pp. 340–60, esp. p. 349.

19. Sukor Kasim, *Study of Strategy*, vol. I, p. 77.

20. See Ch. 6, pp. 148–50.

21. Sukor Kasim, *Study of Strategy*, vol. I, p. 80, footnote 1.

22. Ness, *Bureaucracy and Rural Development*.

23. L. J. Fredericks, *Rural Productivity-raising Strategies and Programmes in Peninsular Malaysia*, Asian and Pacific Development Centre, Kuala Lumpur, 1984, (mimeographed), esp. pp. 48–61.

24. World Bank, *Malaysia: A Review of Fisheries Policies and Programs*, Washington, D.C., 9 November 1983, esp. pp. 29–31.

25. P. T. Bauer, *The Rubber Industry: A Study in Competition and Monopoly*, Harvard University Press, Cambridge, 1948. For a more recent analysis, see Lim Teck Ghee, *Peasants and Their Agricultural Economy in Colonial Malaya 1874–1941*, Oxford University Press, Kuala Lumpur, 1977.

26. These rates are those which were in effect on 18 November 1983, as announced by the Ministry of Finance.

27. See Ch. 2, pp. 30–6.

28. Malaysia Ministry of Finance, *Economic Report 1983/84*, Government Printer, Kuala Lumpur, pp. 168–9.

29. Richard Stubbs, 'Malaysia's Rubber Smallholding Industry: Crisis and the Search for Stability', *Pacific Affairs*, vol. 56, no. 1, 1983, pp. 84–105.

30. Ibid., p. 89.

31. Malaysia, *First Malaysia Plan, 1966–70*, Government Printer, Kuala Lumpur, 1965.

32. S. Selvadurai, *Padi Farming in West Malaysia*, Ministry of Agriculture and Fisheries, Kuala Lumpur, 1972.

33. *Fourth Malaysia Plan*, para. 699, p. 277.

34. Sukor Kasim, *Study of Strategy*, vol. I, pp. 41–2.

35. The Guaranteed Minimum Price of $16 per pikul was raised to $28–$32 per pikul in 1979. *Fourth Malaysia Plan*, para. 116, p. 39.

36. C. L. G. Bell and P. B. R. Hazell, 'Measuring the Indirect Effects of an Agricultural Investment Project on Its Surrounding Region', *American Journal of Agricultural Economics*, vol. 62, no. 1, 1980, pp. 75–86.

37. *Fourth Malaysia Plan*, para. 699, p. 277. See also R. J. G. Wells and L. J. Fredericks, 'Food Policies in Malaysia with Particular Reference to Self-sufficiency and Poverty Reduction Goals', *Kajian Ekonomi Malaysia*, vol. 16, nos. 1 and 2, June–December 1979, esp. pp. 56–60.

38. United Nations Food and Agriculture Organisation, *Production Yearbook*, vol. 34, Rome, 1980.

39. M. Rudner, 'The Malaysian Quandary: Rural Development Policy under the First and Second Five Year Plans' in *Readings on Malaysian Economic Development*, (ed. D. Lim) Oxford University Press, Kuala Lumpur, 1975, p. 64.

40. Vokes, 'Reforming Food Grain Markets', pp. 209–11.

41. Sahathavan Meyanathan, 'Rice Price Control in Malaysia', *Kajian*

Ekonomi Malaysia, vol. 16, nos. 1 and 2, June–December 1979, pp. 223–33.
42. Ibid., p. 224.
43. *Fourth Malaysia Plan*, para. 116, p. 39.
44. Sahathavan, 'Rice Price Control', pp. 224–6. See also, C. P. Brown, 'Rice Price Stabilisation and Support in Malaysia', *Developing Economies*, vol. II, no. 3, 1973.
45. Richard Goldman, 'Staple Food Self-sufficiency and the Distributive Impact of the Malaysian Rice Policy', *Food Research Institute Studies*, vol. 14, no. 3, 1975, pp. 251–93.
46. See p. 48–9 above.
47. 'We Warned LPN, says AG', *Malaysia New Straits Times*, 30 June 1983, p. 1.
48. 'Fertilizer Fiddle: It points to Inside Job', *Malaysia New Straits Times*, 27 September 1982; 'Subsidy Rip-Off: ACA Uncovers Syndicate', *The Star*, 17 January 1983, p. 1.
49. *Malaysia New Straits Times*, 18 February 1982, p. 8.
50. Muda Agricultural Development Authority as quoted in Hing Ai Yun, 'Capitalist Development' in *Ethnicity, Class and Development: Malaysia*, edited by S. Husin Ali, Persatuan Sains Sosial Malaysia, Kuala Lumpur, 1984, p. 324.
51. Affifuddin Haji Omar, 'Some Implications of Farm Mechanisation in the Muda Scheme', *Experience in Farm Mechanisation in South East Asia*, edited by H. Southworth and M. Barnett, 1974. See also D. S. Gibbons *et al.*, *Land Tenure*, esp. pp. 170–3.
52. Vokes ('Reforming Food Grain Markets') reached the conclusion that 'the extent of exploitation (by private middlemen) had been exaggerated', p. 221. Evidence collected from field surveys by Purcal (*Rice Economy*) and Horii (*Rice Economy and Land Tenure*) also supports this conclusion.
53. MTR4MP, pp. 243–5.
54. Colin MacAndrews, *Mobility and Modernization*. For short accounts of FELDA schemes, see Noel Benjamin, 'The Role of Land Settlement in the Economic Development of West Malaysia', *Development and Change*, vol. 9, 1978; Colin MacAndrews and Kasumi Yamamoto, 'Induced and Voluntary Migration in Malaysia', *Southeast Asian Journal of Social Sciences*, vol. 3, 1976.
55. James C. Jackson, *Planters and Speculators. Chinese and European Agricultural Enterprise in Malaya 1786–1921*, University of Malaya Press, Kuala Lumpur, 1968.
56. In fact, one estimate puts the number of applicants at 200,000. See Rokiah Talib, 'The Politics of Land Development in Malaysia', *Manusa dan Masyarakat (Man and Society)*, New Series, vol. 4, 1983, p. 2.
57. For a critical assessment of the Pahang Tenggara project see Benjamin Higgins, 'Perils of Perspective Planning: Pahang Tenggara Revisited', *UNCRD Working Paper no. 79*, 15 December 1979, UN Centre for Regional Development, Nagoya, Japan.
58. For example, under the First Malaysia Plan, 1965–70, the actual annual rate of land development and settlement averaged less than one-third of the planned rate.
59. FELDA: *Annual Report 81*, Kuala Lumpur, p. 12 and Table 8, p. 13.
60. This credit scheme is further discussed on pp. 67–70.
61. Mehmet, 'Evaluating Alternative Land Schemes', p. 344.
62. As a result, FELDA has been facing labour supply problems and has been obliged to rely increasingly on non-resident labour for harvesting. Such labour, typically obtained through labour sub-contractors, sometimes includes illegal Indonesian immigrants and 'red identity card holders', i.e. persons with doubtful citizenship status, utilised under exploitative conditions. A recent notorious scandal was the Selanchar Empat case involving work gangs hired by day and fired by night.

See *Malaysia New Straits Times*, 12 July 1983, p. 2.

63. Mehmet, 'Evaluating Alternative Land Schemes', p. 356.

64. According to one estimate, the size of the 'second generation' population on FELDA schemes is about 0.25 million, or about half the total settler population. See *New Sunday Times*, 23 May 1982.

65. See p. 55.

66. Mehmet, 'Evaluating Alternative Land Schemes'.

67. Information supplied by the Director of Finance, FELDA Head Office.

68. Paul Chan and L. L. Lim, *Case Study of Migrant Settlers in Three Land Schemes in Peninsular Malaysia*, Faculty of Economics and Administration, University of Malaya, Kuala Lumpur, 1981 (mimeo.).

69. '500 FELDA Settlers Stage Protest' (against the block system of tapping), *New Sunday Times*, 17 July 1983; 'Demo at FELCRA Office', *The Star*, 27 August 1982.

70. 'FELCRA settlers lock in office staff', *Malaysia New Straits Times*, 6 April 1982; 'FELCRA Incident: Culprits may face the music', *Malaysia New Straits Times*, 7 April 1982.

71. FELDA *Annual Report 81*, Table 11, p. 14.

72. FELDA *Annual Report 81*; KLSE *Handbook*.

73. 'Ownership Plan for FELDA Settlers', *Malaysia New Straits Times*, 20 April 1984, p. 8.

4 MANAGED INDUSTRIALISATION UNDER TRUSTEESHIP

Introduction

In an important sense, the failure of the Malaysian agricultural and rural development policies to solve rural poverty could be attributed to the phenomenon of 'urban bias'.[1] Under the NEP industrialisation, especially manufacturing, was chosen as the 'leading sector' of the big development push.[2] The objective of the Malaysian strategy of industrialisation was not solely the maximisation of the growth rate. More fundamentally, it was to modernise and urbanise the Malays. This was called socio-economic restructuring 'to reduce and eventually eliminate the identification of race with economic function.'[3] In other words, industrialisation was to be *managed* by trustees to achieve racial balance.

The objectives of managed industrialisation[4] policy were to transform the modern sector in two fundamental ways: (1) to change the racial composition of employment and (2) to restructure the control and ownership of assets on behalf of the Malay community as a whole.

The trustees who managed the NEP industrial policy relied on the tools of state capitalism. On the one hand, they regulated fiscal policy with offers of investment and tax incentives to attract foreign investors. On the other hand, they sponsored the direct participation of the state in the economy by financing public enterprises and specially-created Bumiputera companies (e.g. PERNAS, PNB, UDA, SEDCs, etc), often in joint-ventureship with other investors, both foreign and domestic.

In evaluating the effectiveness of the Malaysian industrial strategy the proper question to ask is: To what extent has industrial restructuring by trusteeship actually uplifted the economic position of the Malays *vis-à-vis* the other Malaysian races? The alternative question, of how rapidly the manufacturing sector has been growing, while not irrelevant, misses the objective of the NEP.

Accordingly the purpose of this chapter is to analyse empirically the socio-economic effects of managed industrialisation under trusteeship. The outline of the chapter is as follows. First, a brief

macro-economic account of the evolution of Malaysian industrialisation, especially in the light of the employment restructuring
targets of the NEP, will be presented. This will be followed by a
more detailed analysis of the labour market impact of managed
industrialisation. The changing trends in asset ownership and
control will be analysed in Chapter 5.

Employment Restructuring and Industrialisation

During the last quarter of a century, but particularly during
1970–80, Malaysia has experienced rapid, and in macro terms a
quite impressive, industrial growth. The manufacturing sector out-
performed the rest of the economy by a substantial margin. It grew
at an annual rate of 11.4 per cent during 1971–80, compared with
the GDP's annual growth rate of 7.8 per cent (in 1970 prices). The
share of the manufacturing sector rose sharply from 13.5 per cent
in 1970 to 18.6 per cent of GDP in 1980 (Table 4.1). After 1980, the
worldwide economic recession led to a slow-down. The GDP
growth rate slowed to 6.2 per cent, and the manufacturing sector
grew only at 4.9 per cent. Its GDP share in 1983 was slightly less
than its 1980 share (Table 4.1).

The Malaysian industrialisation programme can be subdivided
into two phases. In the first phase, covering the period 1958–70,
the dominant strategy was the Import Substitution Industrialisation

Table 4.1: Growth of the Manufacturing Sector, 1970–1983

Item	1970	1980	1983	Average annual growth rate (%) 1971–80	1981–83
GDP at purchaser's value (1970 $ million)	12,308	26,228	31,398	7.8	6.2
Value of manufacturing output (1970 $ million)	1,650	4,875	5,628	11.4	4.9
Share of manufacturing of GDP	13.4	18.6	17.9		
of total employment	11.4	15.6	15.3		
Employment in manufacturing (in thousands)	386.5	750.5	800.3	6.9	2.2

Source: 1970 figures are from: 4MP, Tables 2.1, p. 11 and 4.6, p. 81
        Figures for 1980 and 1983 are from: MTR4MP, Tables 2.1, p. 39 and 4.10,
        p. 127

Table 4.2: The Distribution of Existing Industrial Estates, by States (as at 31 December, 1981)

State	No. of industrial estates	Total area in hectares[a] Planned	Developed	% Developed
Johore	12	1,656.50	1,043.11	63.0
Malacca	7	344.84	266.66	77.3
Negri Sembilan	5	280.05	280.05	100.0
Selangor and F.T.	14	2,253.15	1,762.19	78.2
Perak	6	684.09	537.59	78.6
Penang	8	1,354.85	680.3	50.2
Kedah	6	522.78	459.73	87.9
Perlis	1	13.68	—	—
Pahang	8	1,304.55	635.78	48.7
Trengganu	8	572.20	320.64	56.0
Kelantan	6	621.33	305.26	49.1
Sarawak	5	787.33[b]	700.53	89.0
Sabah	5	374.64	239.16	63.8
Total	91	10,769.99	7,231.04	67.1

Notes: a. Excluding housing
b. Including 96.8 hectares Government area
Source: MIDA *1981 Annual Report*

(ISI), which was then the fashionable strategy of planned development in the Third World.[5] The ISI strategy in Malaysia was vigorously pursued by means of tariff protection, import restrictions and investment incentives offered under the Pioneer Industries Ordinance of 1958. It attracted a large number of branch plants of American, European and Japanese multinational corporations in an effort to start *infant industries*. By the early 1970s, the ISI strategy had reached its limit with about 95 per cent of the consumer durables and 90 per cent of non-durables being produced locally,[6] behind an effective, high rate of protection.[7] Malaysia has moved aggressively into its second-phase of industrialisation, by encouraging export-oriented industries. This, too, has been quite a successful strategy in terms of attracting labour-intensive manufacturing and processing especially in the fields of textiles, garments and electronics. Malaysia now has become the leading exporter of semi-conductors, with an annual gross export value of $2 billion, although the gain in net foreign exchange from this growth is very little, owing to a corresponding increase in the volume of imported parts and components.

One of the key factors behind the relatively successful Malaysian industrialisation drive, has been the establishment of specially-developed industrial estates and free-trade zones.[8] At the end of 1981 there were a total of 91 such estates in the country, with an average of 67.1 hectares (Table 4.2). Collectively these estates accounted for almost half the total employment in the entire manufacturing sector — a proportion virtually certain to increase as there are some 42 new estates proposed under various stages of development.[9]

Table 4.3: Employment Restructuring in Malaysia: Targets and Actual Performance, 1970–80 (in %)

Employment	Malay	Chinese	Indian	Others	Total
1970					
Primary[a]	67.6	19.9	11.5	1.0	100.0
Non-agricultural[b]	38.0	51.3	9.7	1.0	100.0
1980					
Primary	66.3	19.9	13.0	0.9	100.0
Non-agricultural	43.7	45.9	9.6	0.8	100.0
1990					
Targets[c]					
Primary	61.4	28.3	9.6	0.7	100.0
	(59.0)	(29.4)	(10.8)	(0.8)	
Non-agricultural	49.8	38.7	10.8	0.7	100.0
	(48.4)	(40.2)	(10.7)	(0.7)	
Achievement rates 1970–80[d]					
Primary	41.9	0	e	33.3	
Non-agricultural	96.6	85.7	e	66.7	

Notes:
a. Agricultural
b. Non-agricultural sector, consisting of the Secondary and Tertiary sectors, has been used because of definitional differences in the 1970 and 1980 data. For example, in the 3MP, utilities were included in the Secondary sector, while in the 4MP, they are put into the Tertiary sector.
c. There are two sets of employment share targets: the original 3MP targets (Table 4.14, p. 79) and the revised ones in the 4MP (Table 9.5, p. 174). The figures in parentheses refer to the latter.
d. These rates are calculated as follows:

$$At = A - \frac{(T - B)}{2} \times 100$$

where At = achievement rate
     A = actual achievement in employment restructuring 1970–80
     T = 1990 target as set out in TMP
     B = employment share in 1970
e. Indicates a negative achievement

Source: 4MP, Table 3.10, p. 57 and Table 9.5, p. 174; 3MP Table 4.4, p. 79

Ethnic Employment Restructuring: Targets and Performance

The quantitative targets of the policy of ethnic restructuring of employment, to be achieved by 1990, were set out in the *Third Malaysia Plan*[10] as follows:

(1) a sharp decline in the share of Malay employment in the primary sector, dropping from 67.6 per cent in 1970 to 61.4 per cent in 1990;
(2) a correspondingly large increase in the share of Malays in non-agricultural employment, jumping from 38 per cent in 1970 to 49.8 per cent in 1990;
(3) matching shifts in the employment shares of the non-Malay ethnic groups, notably, a greater concentration of the Chinese in the primary sector.

What has been the progress, since 1970 toward the fulfilment of these policy targets? Table 4.3 provides data from the *Fourth Malaysia Plan* which can be utilised to answer this question. Looking at the overall Malay share of non-agricultural employment, it has increased very much along the lines of the NEP forecast. By 1980, this share had risen to 43.7 per cent, while there had been a parallel decline in the Chinese non-agricultural share from 51.3 per cent to 45.9 per cent. Thus, in aggregate terms, it appears that the policy of restructuring of ethnic employment has indeed been working. However, its performance needs to be examined more closely.

Internal Migration

The major impact of the policy of ethnic restructuring was to give rise to a large volume of Malay migration from their traditional rural settlements, called *Kampungs*. During 1970–80, of the 2.4 million people migrating within Peninsular Malaysia, two of every three migrants were Malay and female migrants virtually equalled the number of males (Table 4.4).

Unlike most developing countries, Malaysian rural-to-rural migration was more important than rural-to-urban (Table 4.5), due to two special reasons: (1) a large volume of land development, and (2) the geographical distribution of industrial estates (Table 4.2). In fact, a high proportion of rural industrial workers were *commuters*, residing in *Kampungs* but being bussed to factories on

Table 4.4: Internal Migrants in Peninsular Malaysia, by Sex and Race, 1970–80 (Nos. in thousands)

Race	Male	Female	Total	%
Malay	777.8	760.2	1,538.0	64.5
Chinese	286.5	291.3	577.8	24.2
Indian	132.2	127.1	259.3	10.9
Others	5.5	5.2	10.7	6.4
Total	1,202.0	1,183.8	2,385.8	100.0

Source: Khoo Teik Huat, *1980 Population and Housing Census of Malaysia*, vol. I, Table 5.20, p. 82

Table 4.5: Direction of Internal Migration in Peninsular Malaysia (Nos. in thousands)

| Area of Origin | Area of Destination | | Total |
	Urban	Rural	
Urban	517.5	416.8	934.3
Rural	364.4	1,004.7	1,369.1
Total	881.9	1,421.5	2,303.4

Source: As in Table 4.4, Table 5.17, p. 78

industrial estates. This was especially true in labour-intensive industries, such as electronics, garments and textiles which were particularly responsible for expanding employment and income opportunities.

The Industrial Estates: The Key Formula

The key to industrialisation by trusteeship was the creation of special-purpose Industrial Estates and Free Trade Zones (FTZs), a formula popularised by the United Nations Industrial Development Organisation (UNIDO).

As with other aspects of development by trusteeship in Malaysia, the Industrial Estate formula was utilised by the trustees to good advantage. Its management and implementation is top-heavy and fragmented, providing ample bureaucratic and influence-peddling opportunities.

There are several departments, statutory bodies and state-level authorities involved in various aspects of the programme, without a single centralised agency in charge of overall planning and coordination. The State Development Corporations (SEDCs) are responsible for land acquisition and the maintenance of estates. The Malaysian Industrial Estates Limited (MIEL) provides technical assistance in designing the lay-out of the estates and undertaking the construction of ready-made factory buildings. The Public Works Department, the National Electricity Board and the Telecommunications Department provide infrastructural facilities.

The role of the Malaysian Industrial Development Authority (MIDA) is of special importance. Given these physical facilities, MIDA administers an extensive system of fiscal incentives for investors: (a) Pioneer Status, (b) Labour Utilisation Relief, (c) Locational Incentives, (d) Investment Tax Credit, (e) Export Incentives, (f) Increased Capital Allowances, (g) Hotel Incentives and (h) Special Incentives for Approved Agricultural Industries.[11] By far the most significant of these are the Pioneer Status and Investment Tax Credit incentives. Under the Pioneer Status incentive, total tax exemption from income tax, development tax and excess profit tax is granted for a period of from 2–5 years, depending on the level of fixed capital investment. In addition, an extension of a further year for tax relief is granted to a pioneer factory for each of: (1) location in a development area, (2) production of a priority product or industry, and (3) attainment of a certain local percentage of value-added specified by the Ministry of Commerce and Trade. The amount of tax credit granted under the Investment Tax Credit incentive is not less than 25 per cent of the total capital expenditure, plus an additional 5 per cent credit for each of the conditions (1)–(3).

The administration of the FTZs, which process inputs into parts, components or products for re-exports, is different. Under the enabling Act of 1971 these are to be administered, maintained and operated by an Authority appointed by the Minister of Finance who is advised by an FTZ Advisory Council. In practice, however, the implementation of the FTZ programme involves the same federal and state-level agencies and departments.

In addition to industrial estates and zones, several additional incentives are available to foreign investors. There is monetary stability and a convertible currency. Malaysia has no minimum wages and trade unions are weak and closely controlled by the state with practically no right to strike. The government enforces ethnic job quotas in the context of a cheap labour policy partly with a view to maximising employment opportunities for rural Malays and partly to promote Japanese-style work ethics as part of its *Look East Policy*.[12]

Industrial Estates: The Path to Development or Exploitation?

The strategy of promoting industrialisation based on industrial estates and free trade zones is closely linked with the success story of the 'Gang of Four' countries, South Korea, Taiwan, Hong Kong and Singapore.[13] It represents a highly efficient method of global assembly line toward a new international division of labour. Developing countries, with abundant supplies of cheap labour, are able to utilise imported technology and capital to acquire new comparative advantages to produce price-competitive goods for access to world markets. These comparative advantages are created as a result of economies of scale, due to mass production, and to international marketing, typically channelled through the oligopolistic global distribution networks of multinational corporations[14] or, otherwise, through specially-formed state trading companies.

In the case of Malaysia there is also an important historical explanation for the successful implementation of the global resource assembly converging on industrial estates: *The plantation economy was developed in the same way.* Rubber seeds, risk capital, management expertise and unskilled labour were all imported by colonial authorities to exploit the favourable Malaysian eco-system. Under the colonial administration, much of the plantation profits and surpluses generated by the global resource assembly enriched the foreign interests.[15]

Industrial development in post-Independence Malaysia should, however, benefit, first and foremost, Malaysian citizens. Impoverishment by industrialisation is incompatible with the goals of development, particularly in a rapidly growing country well endowed with resources. The possibility that industrialisation may lead to impoverishment is suggested by the *Dependency Theory*.[16] Some have argued that this theory is applicable to the Malaysian case. How valid is this argument?

A Model of Global Resource Assembly on Industrial Estates

The Malaysian industrial strategy by trusteeship follows neoclassical principles. It is, however, not free enterprise based on the private sector. It is a form of state capitalism. There is a deliberate, often indirect, policy of controlling trade unions to maintain low wages and fringe benefits to achieve international competitiveness and to maximise value added as incentives for potential foreign investors.

Aggregate industrial output, Q, can be conceptualised in terms of a standard production function utilising labour, L, capital, K, technology, T, and land, N:

$$Q = F(L,K,T,N) \tag{1}$$

The environment of production under trusteeship is highly imperfect. In the first place, there are numerous direct and indirect subsidies to imported capital and technological inputs, resulting in distortions in relative factor prices. Also, there are strong non-competitive features in labour markets. Jobs are allocated according to racial quotas, strongly biased in favour of Malays and there are persistent wage differentials. Income distribution is not in accordance with marginal productivity. Influential middlemen derive unearned income as quasi-rents for arranging deals.

However, the production process follows the principles of specialisation and the division of labour, in order to maximise value added, VA, the excess of total revenue, TR, over the total cost of primary inputs, TCPI:

$$VA = TR - TCPI \tag{2}$$

The centrepiece of the production process is the industrial estate, IE. It represents *transnationalisation* of the production process, reflecting a mutually enriching partnership between the Malaysian trustees and foreign investors. Its function is to promote a global resource assembly in the pursuit of specialisation and division of labour.

Figure 4.1 depicts a model of IE as the meeting-place of two resource flows: foreign capital, Kf, and technology, T, and domestic supplies of labour, L, land, N, and capital, Kd. These resources are assembled and processed, utilising transferred technology in pursuit of maximising global value-added. These are then distributed among the various factors of production under conditions of economic exploitation. In labour markets there is monopsony, non-competitive hiring and controlled union activity. Capital and land are heavily subsidised. Therefore, these factors are not paid according to their marginal productivity.

The distribution of value-added parallels the transnationalised

Figure 4.1: A Conceptual Framework of the Global Resource Assembly in Industrial Estates and Free Trade Zones

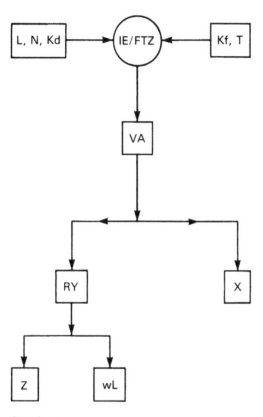

Notations:

IE = Industrial Estates
FTZ = Free Trade Zones
L = Labour
N = Land
Kd = Domestic Capital
Kf = Foreign Capital
T = Technology
VA = Value Added
RY = Retained Income
X = Payments to non-residents
Z = Payments to non-labour input
wL = Wage bill

resource assembly on IE. Just as there are two resource inflows, so there are two outflows of payments from the VA, the share accruing to non-residents, X, and the share accruing to domestic factors, representing retained income, RY. Both X and RY contain elements of the exploitation of factors owing to market imperfections, although

$$VA = RY + X \tag{3}$$

RY is further sub-divided into two components, the share accruing to labour as its wage bill, wL and the share accruing to domestic capitalists and non-labour inputs:

$$RY = wL + s(VA - L) \tag{4}$$

where w and s, respectively, are the marginal wage and non-labour factor costs. Given the market imperfections stated above, it follows that,

$$w \neq F_1 \tag{5}$$

and

$$s \neq F_{k,n,t} \tag{5i}$$

Generally, $w < F_1$ and $s > F_{k,n,t}$ reflecting exploitation of labour by owners of non-labour inputs, both domestic and foreign.

The above conceptualisation is a simple, neo-classical model of production in which resources are mobilised globally for profit-maximisation. Its main focus is on the conflicting interests of the resident and non-resident owners on the one hand, and labour and non-labour factors on the other. More specifically, the objective is to analyse these conflicting interests within a framework of market imperfections resulting in economic exploitation.[17]

The Labour Market Implications of Managed Industrialisation

The above conceptualisation will now be used for an evaluation of the growth of the Malaysian manufacturing industries, focusing on its impact on employment, real wages and poverty.

Table 4.6: Significant Trends in the Manufacturing Sector,
1973–1981

	1973	1981	Average annual growth rate (%) 1973–81
1. Employment:			
— Manufacturing sector	386,500[a]	750,500[b]	6.9[c]
— Manufacturing industries in Peninsular Malaysia[d]	278,935	556,414	9.0
2. Real annual earnings[d] (in 1970 prices):			
— Manufacturing industries in Peninsular Malaysia (before direct tax)	$1,783[e]	$2,532[e]	4.5
— (after direct tax)	$1,713	$2,364	4.0
3. Ratio of wagebill to gross value of sales:			
— Manufacturing industries in Peninsular Malaysia	0.077	0.073	
4. Capital investment per new job[f] (at 1970 prices):	$16,878[g]	$39,541	
5. Employment elasticity of output, 1971–80: 0.61[h]			

Notes and Sources:
   a. = 1970   b. = 1980   c. = 1971–80
   a is taken from 4MP, p. 81; b and c are taken from MTR4MP, p. 127
   d. Source: Dept. of Statistics, Malaysia: *Census of Manufacturing Industries, Peninsular Malaysia*, 1973, Vol. I, Table 1, p. 1 and *Industrial Surveys*, 1981, Table 2.1, p. 35 [which is also a census of Manufacturing Industries]
   e. = Deflated by the GNP deflator of 2.0 for the period 1970–1981. Source: Ministry of Finance, *Economic Report* (various years)
   f. Source: MIDA *Annual Reports*
   g. This figure refers to 1974
   h. $= \dfrac{\text{Annual growth rate (\%) in Manufacturing sector employment}}{\text{Annual growth rate (\%) in Manufacturing sector output}}$

A major difficulty in such an evaluation is the lack of comprehensive and reliable statistics. There are large gaps and inconsistencies in the available sources of data. For example, in the *Fourth Malaysia Plan*, it is estimated that during 1970–80, manufacturing employment grew at an annual average rate of 7.6 per cent, from 386,500 to 803,100. In the latest *Mid-Term Review of the Fourth Malaysia Plan*, the 1980 manufacturing employment has been revised to 750,500 giving a growth rate of 6.9 per cent p.a. during 1970–80 (Table 4.6). The census of manufacturing industries for

1981, which is comparable to the last census in 1973, shows employment in manufacturing industries in Peninsular Malaysia as 556,414. This underestimates the amount by one-third, relative to the figures used by planners — a number too large to be explained by the exclusion of East Malaysian data. Also, the only source of annual, sub-sectoral time-series information (viz. *The Monthly Industrial Statistics* of the Department of Statistics) suffers from limited coverage and other shortcomings.[18] It is based on an establishment survey, only covering about 40 per cent of total manufacturing sector employment relative to the figures of the Fourth Plan. Nevertheless, this source provides consistent (if partial) monthly employment and earnings data since 1973. Utilising this source, along with the census data for 1973 and 1981, reveals a number of significant trends in the growth of the Malaysian manufacturing sector during 1973–1981.

Impressive Macro Performance

First of all, in aggregate terms, there was an impressive rate of growth of employment of 6.9 per cent per annum, according to the *Mid-Term Review of the Fourth Malaysia Plan* or 9.0 per cent per annum according to census data (Table 4.6). Likewise, industry-wide average real earnings (in 1970 prices, and before direct taxes) increased at an average rate of 4.5 per cent during this 8-year period or at 4.0 per cent p.a. after direct taxes.[19] These indicators, as far as they go, compare very favourably with those of other countries.

Capital-intensity and Tariff Protection

At the same time, there are also disturbing macro trends. For example, the employment elasticity of output during 1971–80 was only 0.61, indicating a limited capacity in labour absorption in the growth of the manufacturing sector. This was primarily because of the bias in the investment incentives in favour of capital. Incentives were geared to the size of capital investment thus favouring large, capital-intensive firms, rather than the more labour-intensive, smaller firms.[20] Even when such cases as the Labour Utilisation Relief incentive were designed to encourage labour employment, the incentive was offered merely as an alternative to capital utilisation, and, as a result, had very limited impact on job creation. According to information from MIDA, capital intensity, measured as capital investment per worker, rose 2.3 times during 1974–1981, increasing from $16,878 to $39,541 (in 1970 prices) (Table 4.6).

Thus, the Malaysian industrialisation drive was not only capital-intensive to start with, but it became much more so under the NEP trusteeship. The growth of many new industries, such as electronics, was based on the imports of parts and components accompanied by heavy factor payments abroad, with virtually no backward and forward linkages and minimal local value-added.

By 1970, the limit to import-substitution had practically been reached, and thereafter policymakers stressed export promotion. In 1971 the Free Trade Zone Act was passed under which special incentives were offered to promote export-oriented industries. Nevertheless, import substitution industries producing for domestic consumption remained sheltered behind high effective rates of protection. Thus, motor vehicles, home electrical appliances, plastic products, tyres and tubes, and petroleum and coal products, have required heavy indirect subsidies resulting in the loss of significant employment opportunities. One recent study[21] of the impact of tariff protection on employment in manufacturing industries, estimates that 259,378 jobs would have been created had distortions in the capital market been removed. This is equivalent to 62.7 per cent of the total jobs created in the manufacturing sector during 1970–83. Roughly 80 per cent of these lost jobs would have been in the consumer goods industries. In future, the social cost of protecting import substitution industrialisation may well increase substantially, especially if Malaysia moves into second-generation protection for heavy industries, e.g. the 'Made-in-Malaysia' car project, despite critical advice from economists.[22]

Table 4.7: Employment Trends in Selected Industries, 1973–1982

Industries	Employment June 1973	Employment June 1982	Net Increase	%
Electronics	12,358	79,404	67,046	40.2
Textiles	17,526	36,640	19,114	11.5
Clothing	7,998	21,467	13,469	8.1
Rubber products	9,799	17,924	8,125	4.9
Plywood	12,534	14,832	2,298	1.4
Sub-total	60,215	170,267	110,052	66.1
Total employment in selected manufacturing industries	160,702	327,293	166,591	100.0

Source: Dept. of Statistics, *Monthly Industrial Statistics of West Malaysia*, Tables 4 and 5.

Table 4.8: Average Annual Real Earnings in Manufacturing Industries, Peninsular Malaysia, 1973–81 (in 1970 prices)

Industry (code)	1973	1981	Ratio	Growth Rate p.a.
1. Industry average, before direct tax	$1,783	$2,532	1.0	4.5%
Direct tax rate	3.89%	6.63%		
Industry average, after direct tax	$1,713	$2,364		4.1%
2. Industries below (before-tax basis)				
i. Textiles (32111–32190)		1,841	0.73	
ii. Clothing (32201)		1,529	0.60	
iii. Plywood and particle board mills (33112)		2,062	0.81	
iv. Rubber products and rubber milling off estates (355)		2,369	0.93	
v. Plastics products (35600)		1,982	0.78	
vi. Household radios and related equipment (38320)		2,376	0.94	
3. Industries above (before tax basis)				
i. Motor vehicle bodies (38431)		4,140	1.64	
ii. Assembly of autos and lorries (38432)		3,667	1.45	
iii. Motor vehicle parts (38439)		4,244	1.68	
iv. Tin cans and metal boxes (38191)		2,865	1.13	
v. Brass, copper, pewter and aluminium products (38193)		2,580	1.02	
vi. Iron foundries (37102)		2,782	1.10	
vii. Other iron and basic steel strips (37109)		3,411	1.35	
viii. Pioneer industries n.e.c.		$2,712	1.07	
ix. All other industries covered (31140, 33200, 37101, 37209, 38250, 38291)		$2,822	1.11	

Sources and Methods:

Item 1 has been calculated from the *Census of Manufacturing Industries, Peninsular Malaysia*, 1973, Vol. I, Table 1, p. 35 (which was also a census of manufacturing industries)

Items 2 and 3 are computed from the *Monthly Industrial Statistics of West Malaysia*, June 1981

All prices have been converted to 1970 prices using the GNP deflator taken from *Economic Report* (various years)

Tax rates are from Ismail Salleh cited by I. B. Shari and J. K. Sundaram, 'Income Distribution and the State in Post-Colonial Malaysia', 1983, Table 3.

Sub-industry Employment and Wage Effects

What was the performance of manufacturing industries at the sub-industry level? This is a particularly important question, because it is quite likely that the industry-wide trends conceal significant variations about the observed average rates of growth in employment and real wages. The relevant data are given in Table 4.7, relating to employment growth, and Table 4.8, relating to real earnings.

As many as two out of three new jobs generated by the manufacturing sector appear to have been concentrated in a few labour-intensive industries, such as electronics, textiles and garments (Table 4.7). Real earnings in these industries were significantly below the average for the manufacturing sector as a whole. In the case of clothing, they were only 60 per cent of the industry average. In electronics and rubber products, real earnings were very close to the industry average. On the other hand, in industries requiring generally more skilled labour, such as motor vehicle bodies and parts, assembly of automobiles, real earnings were superior to the industry-wide average (Table 4.8).

Inter-sectoral Poverty Transfer

Thus, the problem of low wages lies in labour-intensive industries, where real earnings in 1981, typically, ranged between $1,500–$2,000 (in constant 1970 prices). Most of these workers are female factory workers. They are also *commuters*, i.e. residing in rural areas but being bussed to factories located on industrial estates.[23]

How can the low earnings in labour-intensive industries be evaluated? Studies by Jamilah Ariffin and others have argued that female factory workers are exploited and subordinated. A more objective test is to compare low wages against the poverty-level of income (PLI) figures. Official PLI figures are not published. If, following Young *et al.*,[24] we take $33 per person per month as the PLI, then a household of five earns a yearly income of $1,980 (in 1970 prices). This implies that a significant proportion of workers from rural areas, working in the manufacturing sector, were earning wages actually below the PLI. Of course, the rural poor working at sub-PLI wages in the manufacturing sector may still be better off compared to their previous income levels, even though they may still be in poverty. Even then, it is evident that the 'trickle-down' effects of the Malaysian industrialisation are spreading very slowly. The trustees have emphasised more the quantity, than the quality, of jobs.

More fundamentally, this pattern of industrialisation may be generating an inter-sectoral transfer of poverty. According to the official poverty figures,[25] during 1970–83 there was increased urban poverty while there was a significant decline in the absolute number of rural poor households (Table 1.2).

Taxation and Forced Savings

A further important aspect of expanding urban poverty under the NEP trusteeship strategy is the role of forced savings. Rural migrant workers are not only confronted with higher costs of living associated with their new employment, they are liable to heavy indirect taxes and higher marginal direct tax rates. In fact, the marginal direct tax rates have risen significantly during 1973–80. Assuming an average income of $1,800–$2,400 before and $4,800–$6,000 after migration (in current prices), the extra tax burden in 1980 would be 6.63 per cent versus 3.89 per cent in 1973 (Table 4.8). In addition, industrial workers are subject to statutory deductions for social security, the proceeds of which are channelled into low-interest-bearing government securities. Overall, taking all forms of taxes in account, the marginal tax rate for earners in the income brackets of $2,000–3,000 is about 25 per cent. By comparison those in the top income brackets are subject to marginal tax rates of only 30–40 per cent.[26]

Malaysia has an impressively high savings-GNP ratio: 21.3 per cent during 1971–75, 28.8 per cent during 1976–80, and 21.6 per cent during the recession years of 1980–83.[27] This can be explained by the burdensome and regressive tax structure whereby indirect taxes and forced savings are levied through social security schemes which pay only nominal benefits. Industrialisation by trusteeship has provided a new and expanding source of savings which, ultimately, are placed under the effective control of the trustees.

The Secondary Labour Market: a Transitory Phenomenon?

The above evidence suggests that the Malaysian industrialisation strategy may have given rise to the emergence of a secondary labour market[28] dominated by low-wage, unskilled or semi-skilled jobs, typically for female factory operatives. Much of the technology transfer has not generated *human capital deepening* through skill upgrading.

The growth of the secondary labour market was not limited to female workers. There was a rapid expansion of casual and un-skilled jobs in the construction and building sectors, resulting significantly from the commercial and institutional building boom which has accompanied urbanisation since 1970. Also, other activi-ties in the informal sector requiring little working capital or techni-cal skills, such as petty trading, hawking and food stalls, grew rapidly in the vicinity of major towns and industrial estates, often using child labour.[29]

Is the secondary labour market phenomenon a transitory phase in the Malaysian industrialisation process? While it is impossible to be categorical on this question, there is ground for pessimism. The Malaysian government recently announced an expansionist popula-tion policy,[30] aimed at achieving 70 million at some unspecified future date. The intention is to accelerate the rate of net growth of the population, currently about 2.0 per cent, thereby increasing both the domestic market and the labour force needed for future industrialisation. However, an expansionary population policy can be expected to reproduce poverty since virtually all of the extra births can be expected among the lower income groups. This expec-tation conforms to the universally observed inverse relationship between *per capita* income and birth rates. The cost of providing additional social services and infrastructure can only add to the burden of the programme of poverty eradication.

An additional reason for perpetuating the secondary labour market in Malaysia is the increasing reliance on imported Indonesian labour, for low-wage employment on estates in the first instance,[31] and subsequently in the modern sector. As these immi-grants get adjusted, usually within six months to a year, they move into the expanding informal urban sectors, working in petty trading or seeking casual employment in the construction industry. This inflow of labour has a generally depressing effect on wages in the modern sector, preventing wage increases much beyond the poverty levels.

Squatter Settlements and Public Housing

After 1970, the secondary labour market was both cause and effect in the growth of squatter settlements in and around the major metropolitan areas of Malaysia. In 1980, according to one estimate, presented in Table 4.9, about one-third of the population in major urban centres lived in squatter settlements. In the Kuala

Table 4.9: Squatter Population in Selected Urban Areas, 1980

(1) Urban Area	(2) Squatter Population	(3) Total Population	(4) (2) as % of (3)
1. KL – Klang Valley	400,000	1,000,000	40
2. Ipoh	60,000	300,000	20
3. Johore Bahru	50,000	200,000	25
4. Prai	20,000	67,000	30
Total	530,000	1,567,000	33.8

Source: Khor Kok Peng, 'The Housing Crisis and the Fourth Malaysian Plan' in *The Fourth Malaysia Plan, Economic Perspectives*, edited by Jomo K. S., and R. J. G. Wells, Malaysian Economic Association, Kuala Lumpur, 1983, p. 144

Lumpur-Klang Valley area — the largest single metropolitan and industrial concentration in the country — the proportion was 40 per cent.

Why did the squatter population increase so rapidly? Clearly the 'urban bias' of the Malaysian development strategy was the overall factor responsible. Within this overall strategy, there were specific policies which directly contributed to the emergence of the squatter problem. Public housing policy was a principal case in point, specifically low-cost housing. Under the *Fourth Malaysia Plan*, about one-third of the total housing allocation was for low-cost housing schemes while most of the allocation went to medium and high-cost housing.[32]

Responsibility for providing low-cost housing specifically for industrial estate workers was delegated to the SEDCs. Indeed, several new, low-cost housing projects near industrial estates have been implemented. However, at the allocation stage, these houses have typically gone to officials and their relatives rather than to industrial workers. In the case of the PKNS, (the Selangor SEDC) housing allocation criteria explicitly gives priority to the agency's own staff based on seniority.[33] In a recent study, it has been estimated that only 20 per cent of the terrace houses and flats constructed by the PKNS, ostensibly for workers at the Ulu Kelang, Sungai Way FTZs and the Shah Alam industrial estates, were actually allocated to them. Most of the houses were given, preferentially, to the PKNS' own employees or their relatives.[34]

Under these circumstances, the migrant workers without connections or sponsors were obliged to seek affordable accommodation in the open market. The disadvantaged are forced to make do with substandard housing in shacks put up on railway cuttings or other vacant land and always subject to eviction.[35] The majority move into squatter settlements where they are subject to exploitation by petty-capitalist landlords profiting from the housing shortage. Thus, in recent years, the steadily rising rural exodus has created a boom in low-quality housing in these settlements, typically made up of corrugated-roof huts and long-houses for renting to factory workers near industrial estates and FTZs.[36]

In the field of public housing, the Malaysian government has been reluctant to follow the lead of Singapore in providing industrial workers with affordable housing. In Singapore, subsidised, low-cost housing has been a major factor contributing to rapid industrial development in a highly egalitarian manner.[37] In Malaysia, housing policy has not been egalitarian. The development of urban real estate, heavily dependent on government housing loans preferentially given to higher-paid officers, has been dominated by speculative developers who have specialised in the more profitable higher-income housing.

Summing Up

In the final analysis, what is the net balance of the Malaysian policy of industrialisation by trusteeship? We shall answer this question by returning to the conceptual framework of Figure 4.1.

Employment of Factors. Quantitatively, there has been an impressive growth of jobs, particularly in labour-intensive industries developed on industrial estates, utilising imported capital and technology. All factors, L, N, Kd, Kf and T have expanded. The capital-labour ratio rose 2.3 times during 1974–81. Thus, the capital utilisation increased faster than the employment of labour, reflecting the fact that Malaysian industrialisation, under the NEP trusteeship, became increasingly capital biased. On this basis, it can be stated that the Malaysian industrialisation policy has rewarded owners of capital and non-labour resources at the expense of workers.

Factor Shares. The most recent data on value-added exist for 1973, so trends in factor shares can only be estimated indirectly from an analysis of gross value of output during the inter-census years 1973–81. As can be seen from Table 4.6, labour's share of gross value of output declined during this period from 7.7 per cent to 7.3 per cent. In after-tax terms, the decline was even higher. Given the emergence of the secondary labour market, characterised by sub-PLI wages, it can also be concluded that many of the migrant workers in the manufacturing sector consisted of the working poor. This is particularly applicable to the Malays who constituted by far the largest group of internal migrants.

Owing to the lack of data, the share of benefits accruing to non-resident factors cannot be precisely determined. Indirectly it can be inferred that it must have increased significantly. Since 1970 there has been a rapid increase in capital intensity in Malaysian industrialisation and the balance of payment figures demonstrate a significant rise in outflows of dividends, profits and interest payments.

Taxation and Forced Savings. The Malaysian tax structure is U-shaped. The upper portion of the U is relatively flat, suggesting that the tax structure is comparatively regressive.[38] Industrial workers, typically in the income brackets of $2,000–3,000, suffer marginal tax rates (inclusive of direct and indirect taxes) of about 25 per cent. In addition they are subject to forced savings under statutory social security and contributory pension schemes. By reducing the take-home pay and the current disposable income of the working groups, these taxes and forced savings further aggravate the problem of the working poor. The following chapters demonstrate that under the system of trusteeship, the control of these savings and tax revenues is directly responsible for elitist wealth accumulation.

External Dependence. To what extent is Malaysia's dependence on a new international division of labour responsible for its poverty problem? Our analysis suggests that owners of foreign capital and technology have certainly derived increasing outflows of profits, dividends and interest payments for their participation in the managed industrialisation under the NEP trusteeship. By itself, however, this does not demonstrate external exploitation due to Malaysia's subordinate status. In fact, since 1970, the role which foreign investment and technology have played in Malaysian industrialisation has been the direct result of the active promotion and encouragement by the NEP trustees who have done so because of self-interest.

Overall then, it can be concluded that, while macro indicators suggest that the Malaysian industrial strategy of trusteeship was quite effective, there is sufficient micro-economic evidence to cast serious doubts on its distributive effects. The evidence suggests that industrialisation generated an inter-sectoral transfer of poverty, particularly for the rural Malay migrants, as a result of low wages. While these working poor might have been in greater poverty prior to migration, there is too marginal an improvement in that economic status to justify calling the Malaysian policy of industrialisation by trusteeship a success story. Additionally, tax revenues and forced savings from labour's share of income, which are mobilised for accumulationist equity restructuring under the control of trustees, represent another serious cause of concern about the contribution of Malaysian industrialisation toward poverty redressal.

Notes

1. Michael Lipton, *Why Poor People Stay Poor: Urban Bias in World Development*, M. Temple Smith Ltd., London, 1977.

2. P. N. Rosenstein-Rodan, 'Problems of Industrialisation of Eastern and South-eastern Europe', *Economic Journal*, vol. 53, 1943, pp. 202–11.

3. *Third Malaysia Plan*, para. 27, p. 7.

4. Ozay Mehmet, 'Managed Industrialisation and Poverty Redressal Policies in Malaysia', *South East Asian Economic Review*, vol. 1, no. 3, December 1980. Reprinted in *The Malaysian Economy and Finance*, edited by Sritua Arief and Jomo K. Sundaram, Rosecons, East Balmain, N.S.W., Australia, 1983, pp. 36–49.

5. C. Zuvekas, *Economic Development, An Introduction*, Macmillan, New York, 1981.

6. Chee Peng Lim, *et al.*, 'The Case for Labour Intensive Industries in Malaysia' in *The Development of Labour Intensive Industry in ASEAN Countries*, edited by Rashid Amjad, ARTEP/ILO, Geneva 1981, p. 255.

7. See pp. 87–8.

8. Mrinal Datta-Chaudhuri, *The Role of Free Trade Zones in the Creation of Employment and Industrial Growth in Malaysia*, ARTEP/ILO, Bangkok, 1982.

9. Malaysian Industrial Development Authority, *Annual Report, 1981*, Kuala Lumpur.

10. *Third Malaysia Plan*, Table 4.4, p. 79; *Fourth Malaysia Plan*, Table 3.10, p. 57 and Table 9.5, p. 174.

11. Ministry of Finance, Malaysia: *Economic Report 1983/84*, National Printing Department, Kuala Lumpur, pp. 199–201.

12. Wendy Smith, 'Japanese Factory — Malaysian Workers' in *The Sun Also Sets: Lessons in Looking East*, edited by K. S. Jomo, Insan, Kuala Lumpur, 1983. On the Look East Policy, see MRT4MP, p. 25.

13. Eddy Lee, (ed.), *Export-Led Industrialisation and Development*, Asian Employment Programme, ILO, Geneva, 1981.

14. Gerald K. Helleiner, *International Economic Disorder*, University of Toronto

Press, 1981., Richard J. Barnet and Ronald E. Muller, *Global Reach, the Power of Multinational Corporations*, Simon and Schuster, New York, 1974.

15. J. J. Puthucheary, *Ownership and Control of the Malayan Economy*, Eastern Universities Press, Singapore, 1960; Douglas S. Pauuw and John C. H. Fei, *The Transition in Open Dualistic Economy, Theory and Southeast Asian Experience*, Yale University Press, New Haven, Conn., 1973.

16. S. Amin, G. Frank, C. Bettleheim, I. Wallerstein and others.

17. Ozay Mehmet, 'Growth and Impoverishment in an Open Dual Economy with Capital Imports', *Australian Economic Papers*, vol. 22, 1983, pp. 221–32.

18. For example, small-scale industries are excluded. On the importance of the latter, see Chee Peng Lim, 'A Study of the Patterns of Employment and Wages in Small Industry in Malaysia', *Developing Economies*, vol. XVI, no. 1, 1978, pp. 34–53.

19. In addition to direct taxes, there are statutory deductions for social security and, more recently, new forms of forced savings, such as the National Unit Trust Scheme (ASN) whereby private employers are required to make pay deductions to facilitate worker participation in the ASN. This scheme is discussed in greater detail in Ch. 5.

20. N. D. Karunaratne and M. B. Abdullah, 'Incentive Schemes and Foreign Investment in the Industrialisation of Malaysia', *Asian Survey*, vol. 17, no. 3, 1978, pp. 261–74.

21. Tan Siew Ee and Lai Yew Wah, 'Employment Impact of Tariff Protection: A Case Study of West Malaysian Manufacturing Industries' in *The Fourth Malaysia Plan, Economic Perspectives*, edited by Jomo K. Sundaram and R. J. G. Wells, Malaysian Economic Association, Kuala Lumpur, 1983, p. 135.

22. Chee Peng Lim, 'The Malaysian Car Industry at the Crossroads: Time to change gear?' in *The Malaysian Economy at the Crossroads: Policy Adjustment or Structural Transformation*, edited by Lim Lin Lean and Chee Peng Lim, Malaysian Economic Association, Kuala Lumpur, 1984, pp. 437–54. Osman Rani Hassan, 'New Directions in Industrialisation: Some Strategic Issues', paper presented at the Seminar on *The Mid-Term Review of the Fourth Malaysia Plan*, organised by Persatuan Ekonomi Malaysia on 17 May 1984 (mimeo.).

23. Perunding Bersatu, *The Development of Industrial Estates — An Evaluation and Impact Study*, Main volume, 1983, Kuala Lumpur; Jamilah Ariffin, 'Impact of Modern Electronics Technology on Women Workers in Malaysia: Some Selected Findings From the HAWA Survey', paper presented at the International Symposium on Technology, Culture and Development, University of Malaya, 13 December 1983, Kuala Lumpur (mimeo.).

24. In Kevin Young, *et al., Malaysia: Growth and Equity in a Multiracial Society*, Johns Hopkins University Press, Baltimore, 1975, p. 129. A cutoff line of $43 household *per capita* income in 1974 was used. Using a GNP deflator during 1970–74, viz. 1.32, the figure of $43 in 1974 is converted into $33 in 1970 prices. It is important to add that the Malaysian Plans do not specify the poverty-level-income on which official poverty figures are based.

25. MT4MP, Table 3.2, p. 80.

26. Ismail Mohd. Salleh, 'Sources, Performance and Incidence of Taxation in Malaysia' in *The Malaysian Economy and Finance*, edited by Sritua Arief and Jomo K. Sundaram, Rosecons, East Balmain, N.S.W., Australia, 1983, particularly Table 8, pp. 110–11.

27. FMP, Table 2.5, p. 26; MT4MP, Table 2.3, p. 46.

28. P. Doeringer and M. Piore, *Internal Labour Markets and Manpower Analysis*, Heath, Lexington, Mass., 1971.

29. A. E. Lai, 'The Little Workers: A Study of Child Labour in the Small-scale Industries of Penang', *Development and Change*, vol. 13, no. 4, 1982, pp. 565–85.

P. J. Rimmer, D. W. Drakakis-Smith, and T. G. McGee (eds), *Food, Shelter and Transport in Southeast Asia and the Pacific*, Department of Human Geography, Monograph 12, Australian National University, 1978.

30. MT4MP, para. 59. pp. 21–2.

31. See Ch. 2, pp. 25–6.

32. 4MP, Table 22–3, p. 368.

33. 'Buy up, rent out scandal at PKNS', *Malaysia New Straits Times*, 21 January 1984, p. 6.

34. Susan Lee, 'Industrialisation and the Squatter Phenomenon in the Kelang Valley: Case Studies of Migrant Women Factory Living Conditions', paper presented at the International Symposium on Technology, Culture and Development, 13 December 1983, University of Malaya, Kuala Lumpur, esp. p. 6.

35. 'Squatter Woes', *The Star*, 9 February 1984, p. 22.

36. Michael Johnstone, 'Housing Investment, Savings and Capital Accumulation in Urban Squatter Settlements in Malaysia', *Manusa dan Masyarakat*, New Series, vol. 4, 1983, pp. 38–46.

37. During 1960–79 the Housing Development Corporation built a total of 357,413 units of public housing, at an average annual rate of 18, 502. Jon S. T. Quah, 'Public Bureaucracy, Social Change and National Development' in *Singapore Development Policies and Trends*, edited by Peter S. J. Chen, Oxford University Press, Singapore, 1983, p. 203.

On the contribution of public housing to reducing income inequality, see V. V. Bhanoji Rao and M. Ramakrishnan, *Income Inequality in Singapore*, Singapore University Press, Singapore, 1980, esp. Ch. 5.

38. Ismail Mohd. Salleh in *The Malayan Economy and Finance*.

PART THREE: WEALTH CONCENTRATION UNDER THE NEP

5 WEALTH CONCENTRATION UNDER TRUSTEESHIP: CORPORATE AND HUMAN CAPITAL

Introduction

The paramount objective of the New Economic Policy was wealth restructuring. Wealth differs from income as stock does from flow. As a stock, wealth consists of physical capital, (e.g. machinery, real estate) corporate assets and human capital, embodied in the acquired skills and specialised knowledge of workers. All of these various forms of wealth have the common characteristic of generating a stream of net income. This income represents the yield, over a finite length of time, of an initial investment incurred by the investor.

For historical reasons associated with Malaysian colonialism, the ownership and control of both corporate and human capital had been largely in foreign hands. At the start of the NEP, foreign residents owned or controlled almost two-thirds of total corporate assets, while Bumiputera individuals and trust agencies accounted for only 3.4 per cent, and the other Malaysian residents (mostly Chinese) shared 34 per cent (Table 5.1). As far as human capital was concerned, Puthucheary[1] and others had shown that, at the time of Independence, practically all of the senior staff of agency houses, banks and the colonial establishment were British and European, creating an invisible drain on the country's balance of payments.

The restructuring objective of the NEP was designed to get rid of excessive foreign control and ownership. Simultaneously it attempted to rectify the popular (but exaggerated) perception of the Chinese domination of industry and commerce.[2] It was determined that the Malay community, *as an ethnic group*, should increase its share of corporate assets to 30 per cent by 1990 in comparison to 40 per cent for the other Malaysians and 30 per cent for non-residents.

Likewise, the NEP aspired to a similar restructuring of human capital by means of a comprehensive strategy of employment restructuring. In order to prepare Malays for employment in the modern sector, the government launched a massive programme of

Table 5.1: Ownership of Share Capital in the Corporate Sector,
1971–83 (in %)

	1971	1975	1980	1983
1.0 Malaysian residents	38.3	46.7	57.1	66.4
1.1 Bumiputera individual and trust agencies	4.3	9.2	12.5	18.7
1.11 Bumiputera individuals	2.6	3.6	5.8	7.6
1.12 Bumiputera trust agencies	1.7	5.6	6.7	11.1
1.2 Other Malaysian residents	34.0	37.5	44.6	47.7
2.0 Foreign residents	61.7	53.3	42.9	33.6
2.1 Share in Malaysian companies	32.9	31.3	24.0	18.2
2.2 Net assets of local branches	28.8	22.0	18.9	15.4

Sources: For 1971 and 1975: 4MP, Table 3.14, p. 62
     For 1980 and 1983: MTR4MP, Table 3.12, p. 101

investment in the development of human resources through an expanded system of higher education and scholarships for university studies at home and abroad.

Of course, the timing of the NEP policy of wealth restructuring was not accidental. It came in the aftermath of the May 1969 race riots immediately after a general election which went badly for the Malays. Violence followed the widespread Malay dissatisfaction with Tunku Abdul Rahman's Alliance government's policy of accommodation during the first dozen years of Independence.[3] As well, it was a policy in tune with the wave of economic nationalism of the newly-independent Third World countries aspiring to indigenise capital and employment. However, in multi-racial Malaysia, the brand of economic nationalism adopted was ethnic-based and restricted to Malay nationalism, excluding others.

Trusteeship was the chosen policy instrument of wealth restructuring. Originally a small group of top political/bureaucratic leaders, inspired by Tun Razak, simply assumed the role of political trustees (i.e. guardians) of the Malay community. To accomplish the objective of 30 per cent equity restructuring, this leadership conceived of the institution of *Bumiputera Trust Agencies*, as special-purpose public enterprises, acquiring equity in the name and on behalf of the *rakyat*. Compared to the alternatives of nationalism or confiscation, equity restructuring by trusteeship offered a piecemeal yet pragmatic solution to the traditional Malay state of capitalist underdevelopment. Under this formula, the 30 per cent target was subject to a 20-year sunset clause and control was totally divorced from ownership. Equity and portfolio control was entrusted to (more properly assumed by) the trustees, while ownership was nominally (or better still artificially) and collectively assigned to the Bumiputera community without specifying any date or means of divestiture.

With the NEP trusteeship period approaching its end, what has been the impact of wealth restructuring since 1970? Regarding corporate assets, the latest official figures show that, by 1983, the Bumiputera individuals and trust agencies owned 18.7 per cent of the total share capital in the corporate sector, while other Malaysians accounted for 47.7 per cent, and foreign residents for 33.6 per cent (Table 5.1). In fact, however, the Bumiputera share of 18.7 per cent is almost certainly understated owing to definitional problems in the official data. For example, nominee companies are included in the share of other Malaysians. Yet, it is well-known that a significant proportion of such companies are owned by Bumiputeras. Overall, then, it appears that the wealth restructuring policy objective of 30-30-40 is being achieved very much on target.

The fundamental problem with the NEP policy of wealth restructuring is not so much its overall objective, or the rate of its progress. It is with its redistributive effects. Who is it really benefiting? In theory, it is supposed to eliminate the historical economic disadvantage of the Malays as an ethnic group.

In practice, is the trusteeship system actually succeeding in transferring wealth to the *rakyat*? The purpose of this chapter is to examine this question. The chapter is organised in four sections. Following this introduction, Section II will examine the mobilisation of savings as a prelude to an empirical analysis of the trends in the policy of equity restructuring in Section III. Section IV will review the process of human capital formation in the Malaysian university system, based on a large-scale survey of graduates conducted in 1983.

Mobilisation of Savings for Equity Restructuring

The first necessary condition of equity restructuring under trusteeship is a successful mobilisation of savings. Accordingly, the Malaysian monetary policy is designed to promote thrift and savings for national development.[4]

Monetary Policy and Public Debt

The Bank Negara Malaysia has done a competent job in promoting a strong and convertible currency, a healthy balance of payments position and a reasonable level of price stability. In turn, these factors have been quite instrumental in Malaysia's relative success in attracting foreign investment for its industrialisation drive.

Traditionally, Malaysia has maintained a favourable merchandise trade balance, more than adequate to offset the services deficit. With the launching of the NEP in 1970, and particularly after 1976, there has been a significant increase in net borrowing, both from external and domestic sources. The servicing of foreign borrowing, in the form of profits, interest and dividends, more than doubled during 1976–82. This has been a major factor contributing to the reversal of the current account and the overall balance from one of surplus to one of deficit.[5] In direct consequence of such large-scale acquisitions as Sime Darby and Guthrie's during 1980–82, net foreign borrowing rose from 3.2 per cent to 8.3 per cent of the GNP (Table 5.2), although currently Malaysia has no foreign servicing debt problems. Net domestic borrowing also rose dramatically under the NEP trusteeship system. Furthermore, domestic borrowing and debt management are subject to political pressures despite resistance by technocrats in charge of monetary policy. This reflects the paramount objective of the leadership in

Table 5.2: Indicators of Monetary Policy, 1970–82

	1970	1976	1980	1983
1. Merchandise Trade Balance, f.o.b.	+ 1.0	+ 3.7	+ 4.9	− 1.9
2. Services balance	− 0.8	− 2.1	− 4.9	− 5.5
of which investment income	− 0.4	− 1.1	− 1.8	− 2.3
3. Current account balance	+ 0.2	+ 1.5	0.0	− 7.6
4. Overall balance	+ 0.6	+ 2.1	+ 1.0	− 0.6
5. Net domestic borrowing	0.3	1.7	3.7	6.0
6. Net foreign borrowing	0.3	0.5	1.6	4.9
7. Net foreign borrowing as % of GNP	−	−	3.2	8.3
8. Malaysian ringgit per US$	3.08	2.54	2.22	2.32
9. CPI (1967 = 100), Peninsular Malaysia	101.3	147.8	179.5	208.4

Note: − = Negligible
Source: Ministry of Finance, Malaysia, *Economic Report* (various years)

charge of the NEP trusteeship of mobilising and channeling savings, including forced savings, into wealth restructuring, irrespective of the requirements of an efficient monetary policy.[6]

Savings Mobilisation. The mobilisation of savings has been an effective strategy as evidenced from the impressive aggregate rate of savings achieved since 1970. In particular, the NEP trustees have successfully tapped forced savings from such traditional and low-cost sources of institutional savings as the Employees' Provident Fund (EPF) and the Social Security Organisation (SOCSO). Furthermore, in recent years, these have been supplemented by Islamic saving drives to encourage deposit accounts among the intensely religious grass-roots. The Malaysian institutional network of savings mobilisation also includes pension and cooperative saving societies such as the Armed Forces and other professional groups as well as political parties, notably the Malaysian Chinese Association.[7] Surplus funds accumulated through this large-scale saving network are channelled via a rapidly expanding network of banking and financial institutions to finance equity restructuring under the trusteeship system.

Growth of Banks and Financial Companies

Equity restructuring has been a boon to banks and financial companies, particularly to the Bumiputera-controlled and owned institutions launched by the government to implement this policy. Since the inauguration of the NEP, the number of commercial

Table 5.3: Classification of Commercial Banks by Total Assets, 1972–82 (million $)

Total Assets	1972	1982
Less than 50	15	—
50–99	8	3
100–199	6	1
200–299	2	5
300–499	2	8
500–999	4	9
1000 and Over	—	12
Total	37	38

Source: Bank Negara *Quarterly Economic Bulletin*, June 1983, Table 1.22, p. 43.

Table 5.4: Classification of Finance Companies by Total Assets, 1972–82 (million $)

Total Assets	1972	1982
Less than 20	20	2
20– 49	7	6
50– 99	2	6
100–200	2	11
200 and Over	—	15
Total	31	40

Source: Bank Negara *Quarterly Economic Bulletin*, June 1983, Table 1.23, p. 43.

banks has remained virtually unchanged. There has been a significant change in the composition and the structure of the financial
sector. The country's two leading banks — the Bank Bumiputera
and the United Malayan Banking Berhad — are government institutions. There has also been a significant trend toward concentration in this sector. Whereas in 1972, most of the banks were
relatively small — 40 per cent had assets of less than $50 million —
by 1982 no bank had assets of this size and only three had assets less
than $100 million (Table 5.3). Even more remarkable was the
growth and concentration in finance companies. During the same
period they increased in numbers as well as in total assets (Table
5.4).

Institutional Savings: New and Old Sources

Two of the most important sources of institutional savings providing liquidity for general development financing are the EPF and
SOSCO.[8]

The Employees' Provident Fund (EPF) was originally established in 1951 as a contributory pension scheme. It has been an
extremely successful operation, accumulating large annual net surpluses. Under Malaysian law, these surpluses have been invested in
low-interest-bearing, long-term government securities. During the
30 years ending in 1981, EPF collected $6.8 billion from its contri-
butors — mostly lower-income workers — plus $4.0 billion in
investment income. It invested a total of $10.2 billion in govern-
ment securities.[9]

The Malaysian Social Security Organisation (SOSCO), started in
1971, was established to provide death and disability benefits to
cover workers earning less than $500 per month. It, too, has

managed to accumulate large surpluses, which by law have also been invested in low-interest-bearing, long-term government securities. One important reason for its successful accumulation of surpluses has been its miserly record of benefit payments. During the period 1971–80, SOSCO collected $243 million from its subscribers but paid an estimated $23.5 million as benefits, or a dismal 10 per cent. Its accumulated annual surpluses enabled its asset position to grow to $360 million at the end of 1981.[10]

Islamic Savings: The Tabung Haji

One manifestation of the recent resurgence of Islam has been the establishment of Islamic banks and saving institutions, promoting national thrift and mobilising funds for equity restructuring. We shall now examine Lembaga Urusan dan Tabung Haji (LUTH) or the Pilgrims' Management and Fund Board, one of the oldest and most successful of the Islamic institutions that has emerged as an important institutional saver for equity restructuring.

Tha Tabung Haji, as it is popularly known as, combines Malay capitalism and religion in a uniquely Malaysian way. On the one hand, it encourages Malay savings in deposit accounts from those devout Moslems intending to go on a pilgrimage to Mecca, providing travel and related tourist services. On the other, it channels savings thus generated into highly diversified and rapidly accelerating corporate growth. This capitalist role, in association with both local investors and multinational corporations, now covers manufacturing, plantation and real estate sectors. It has come about directly because of the opportunities provided under the NEP trusteeship target of 30 per cent Bumiputera equity ownership. This will be demonstrated in the next chapter.

At the end of 1981, depositors, spread over Malaysia, numbered 470,000 and had total deposits of $628 million.[11] The average deposit was $1,336 or about 26 per cent of the $5,000 required before the depositor can qualify for pilgrimage under the Board's auspices. The Board does not offer its depositors any loan or financial assistance, but does pay *Zakat*, the religious tax.

The Board's performance as an investor has been spectacular. Its investment policy has been in the hands of a committee of professional bankers and financial experts. Thanks to its privileged links with the government and the Ministry of Commerce and Industry, it has been able to enter into a number of profitable equity restructuring deals with multinational corporations. At the end of 1983,

LUTH had equity interests in no less than 27 public companies listed on the Kuala Lumpur Stock Exchange (KLSE). It owned 50.1 million shares or 9.6 per cent of the total stocks in the top 145 public companies included in our special survey (see below) and as such, it was the 22nd largest stockholder in this survey (Tables 5.7).

During the financial year 1983 LUTH's net profit was $33.1 million, from which $2.7 million was paid as '*Zakat*', $17.4 million was paid out as bonus to depositors — at the rate of 8.5 per cent, virtually identical to the interest on 1-year fixed term deposits in non-Islamic banks — and the remaining $13 million, or 39.2 per cent, was put into the reserve fund to finance further investment actitivity. In the course of 1983, a total of $75.1 million was utilised from the Board's accumulated reserves for equity and real estate investments.[12]

It is evident that the Tabung Haji has placed further corporate growth before the interests of its depositors. Its bonus policy has been consistently conservative, while the lion's share of its annual net profits has been diverted into the reserve fund to finance acqui-sitions and investment growth. Thus, there is a basic conflict of interest between the depositors and the LUTH organisation. In the process, it is emerging as one of the country's key corporate bodies, thanks to its ability of mobilising the savings of its depositors in its role as a trustee agency.

The National Unit Trust Scheme (ASN)

The unit trust scheme known as the Amanah Saham Nasional (ASN) is an even larger system of mobilising Malay savings for equity restructuring. It was launched in 1981, with a lot of fanfare, as a major vehicle for implementing the transfer of corporate assets held under trusteeship to the *rakyat*. In fact in its implementation and design it has become a large-scale deposit saving scheme.

First, it is relevant to detail some of the institutional sequence of events leading to the establishment of the ASN. In January 1978 the Bumiputera Investment Foundation was incorporated to for-mulate policies and guidelines for Bumiputera equity investment participation. In March 1978 the National Equity Corporation (Permodalan Nasional Berhad — PNB) was incorporated as a wholly-owned subsidiary of the Foundation. PNB is a commercial organisation, managed by professionals who are responsible for selecting and operating the portfolio of shares of limited companies in Malaysia to be held in trust for subsequent sale to individual

Bumiputera investors. In May 1979, the ASN was incorporated as a wholly-owned subsidiary of the PNB for the purpose of marketing units to Bumiputera investors and managing the trust fund.[13]

To launch the ASN, Bumiputera companies (e.g. PERNAS) and statutory bodies (e.g. SEDCs) were required by the government to sell part of their equity portfolios, at book value, to the PNB. Thus, in 1982, PERNAS reported a substantial loss for the year because it had been obliged to transfer over $1 billion worth of assets to the PNB.[14] This government-imposed sale of assets encountered strong opposition from PERNAS and other affected Bumiputera interests.[15]

Participation in the ASN is restricted to Malays 18 years of age and over. Some non-Malays who are employees of certain organisations are entitled to purchase ASN units. They are numerically insignificant.

Some of the principal features of the ASN are now examined in greater detail.

Separation of Ownership and Control. The ASN scheme is based on a clear separation of equity ownership and corporate control. Ownership is fairly widely distributed among 1.5 million Bumiputera investors (i.e. unit-holders) but they do not have the right to appoint or change the managers. Immediate control as distinct from ultimate control,[16] including decisions regarding the investment portfolio, rests with a management team appointed by the PNB and the Bumiputera Investment Foundation. In theory, the unit-holders can remove any manager by calling a special meeting. But there are stiff conditions. It must be requested by no less than 50, or 10 per cent of the unit-holders, whichever is less, and mobilise no less than 75 per cent of the voting power vested with registered unit-holders in order to support a motion for the removal of any manager.[17] In practice, these provisions ensure that corporate control remains beyond the hands of the unit-holders, immediately with the ASN, PNB and the Bumiputera Investment Foundation, and ultimately with the Bumiputera elite who monopolise the political and economic power at the centre.

Ability-to-pay Principle. Participation in the ASN scheme is based on the ability-to-pay principle. However, to make the scheme affordable to poor Malays, low-cost loans are available. Workers are encouraged and employers are coaxed to undertake payroll

Table 5.5: Participation in the National Unit Trust Scheme

1. Eligible Bumiputera investors (No.)	4,647,309
2. Unit-holders as at January 1984 (No.)	1,482,396
3. Participation rate as at January 1984 (%)	31.9
4. Total cumulative investment as at January 1984 ($ mil.)	1,269.7
5. Total cumulative redemption as at January 1984 ($ mil.)	246.9
6. Average value of investment per participant ($)	857

Source: Amanah Saham Nasional Berhad, 21 February 1984, Kuala Lumpur

deductions for the purchase of ASN units. Nevertheless, the ability to pay is a major barrier. Moreover, this condition seems to run counter to the original idea of trusteeship in the name of the Malay community. Implicit in the trusteeship formula was the expectation that the wealth, accumulated and held in trust, would ultimately be distributed on the basis of ethnic membership rather than on the basis of affordability. The ASN's ability-to-pay principle is also counter to the subsidy method of financing equity restructuring, originally launched under the trusteeship.

Although the units are priced at $1, they are only available in $100 denominations or more, up to maximum of $50,000 per investor. To encourage small-scale participation, funds can be accumulated in saving accounts at places of work or at the post office. The ability-to-pay principle has effectively reduced the degree of participation in the scheme. Thus, by January 1984, only 31.9 per cent of the eligible Bumiputera population of 4.65 million had participated in the ASN, with an average value per unit-holder of $857 (Table 5.5), but this last figure is misleading since there is a very large variation around this average.

Investment Yield or Capital Gains? Under a normal unit trust fund the unit-holder, as a risk-taker, can expect to make capital gains in addition to a certain level of investment yield as dividend. In fact, it is the prospect of capital gains rather than investment yield which is the typical motivation behind participation.

Under the ASN scheme unit-holders can only resell their units to the fund at the original par value of $1. This condition, in force until 1990, has been justified as allowing ASN to build a strong equity base. In actual fact, it is a regressive formula highly burdensome for the small savers. For example, redemptions up to January 1984 amounted to about 20 per cent of accumulated investments. These are typically from small investors who cash in to meet current economic or social obligations. By so doing, they not only suffer capital loss but they also cross-subsidise others. The large capital gains anticipated in 1990 are unlikely, given the fact that, at that time, there may well be a rush to sell and few willing buyers, forcing a big devaluation of the units.

By way of compensation for the separation of ownership and control, unit-holders have been guaranteed a minimum annual dividend of 10 per cent until 1990. In addition, the first $4,000 of investment income is tax-exempt resulting in an effective yield of up to 15 per cent.[18] In bullish stock markets, ASN units have done well. Bonus issues were declared in 1980 and 1982 of 1 for 10 and 1 for 12.5 respectively.[19] While all these features appear to be positive, they do not remove the ability-to-pay obstacle for the typical rural Malay. For those who can afford to participate but wish to cash in their capital gains before 1990, there is an incentive to discount the units through blackmarket transactions. Those who wait patiently for 1990 may well be disappointed, unless an effective remedy is found for preventing a rush to sell without enough buyers.

All in all, the ASN is a relatively attractive savings scheme. It is not a method of divesting the corporate assets which have been acquired in the name of the Malays and placed under the direct control of the NEP trustees.

Concentration of Ownership of Corporate Assets

In order to test empirically the impact of the NEP trusteeship on the ownership of corporate assets in Malaysia, stockholding data of the corporations registered in Malaysia and listed on the Kuala Lumpur Stock Exchange (KLSE) were analysed. The KLSE publishes an annual *Handbook* which contains a comprehensive list of all corporations that are its members. This membership includes not only companies registered in Malaysia but also a number that are registered in Singapore and elsewhere. For the analysis below, only those registered in Malaysia were selected from the latest *Handbook*, containing corporate information as at the end of 1983.

Coverage and Selection Criteria

The largest corporations were selected. The criterion of size was the latest paid-up capital as shown in the 1983 *Handbook*.[20]

An important objective of this analysis was to compare these results with those obtained in earlier studies, in order to determine trends in asset ownership under the NEP. For this purpose, the Lim study[21] was selected, since his industrial coverage was comprehensive whereas Sieh's[22] was limited to only the manufacturing sector. However, both related to the same time, 1974–75. In Lim's study, a total of 62 top companies were studied (38 had to be excluded because of the lack of relevant data) and the top 25 stockowners in each of these companies were identified. As a result of multiple stockholdings, there were only 797 shareholders selected.

Accordingly, the test required identification of the top 797 stockowners of the largest corporations in all sectors of the economy at the end of 1983. The overall aim was to evaluate trends in the concentration of ownership of corporate assets from 1974–5 to 1983. The fact that the individuals composing the set of 797 might now be different was deemed secondary to the objective of determining whether or not this set's share of ownership was larger or smaller.

There were some minor differences between this study and Lim's. We were unable to identify the top 25 shareholders in each company since the KLSE 1983 *Handbook* only identified the top 10. This meant that we had to cover a larger set of companies than he did in order to reach the target of 797. In fact, a total of 145 companies were covered (see Appendix, Table 5A.1), because, as in earlier studies, we were unable to obtain relevant information for a good number of companies (see Appendix, Table 5A.2). Even attempts at tracing ownership data from the files of the Registrar of Companies in Kuala Lumpur, where by law such information should be available, proved futile.[23] Since the stock of most of the excluded companies was thought to be owned by the top stockholders, this exclusion, as in previous studies, tends to understate the measured concentration ratio. Another factor tending to understate inequality is that our sample of 145 companies excludes private companies, Bumiputera companies and wholly-owned subsidiaries, a number of which (e.g. Bank Bumiputera, PERNAS, PETRONAS) are owned by the government, while some belong to larger corporate stockowners.

The Results: Increased Wealth Concentration

Theoretically, assuming there was no multiple stockownership, there would be a maximum of 1,450 stockowners of the 145

Table 5.6: Size Distribution of Shares among the Top 797 Shareholders in the Largest Corporations in Malaysia, 1983 and 1974–5

% of share shareholders		Number of shareholders	No. of 1983 shares (in billions)	% of Shares held	
				1983	1974–75
Bottom	20%	159	0.010	0.20	0.40
Next	30%	240	0.090	1.72	2.16
Next	10%	79	0.081	1.56	1.30
Next	10%	80	0.134	2.58	2.41
Next	10%	79	0.249	4.78	4.72
Next	10%	80	0.596	11.46	13.28
Next	5%	40	0.7655	14.72	12.70
Next	4%	32	1.5996	30.75	33.88
Top	1%	8	1.677	32.23	29.15
Total		797	5.202	100.00	100.00
Gini Coefficient[a]				.83	.84

Note: a. Calculated by the formula: $G = 1 - \sum_{i=1}^{n} (f_i - f_{i-1})(y_i + y_{i-1})$

where: f_i = % of total number of shareholders in the ith group

y_i = % of total number of shares held by the ith group

Sources: 1983 KLSE *Annual Companies Handbook*, Vol. IX
1974–75 Lim Ma Hui, *Ownership and Control*, Table 3.8, p. 29

corporations selected for study. In fact, however, multiple ownership is very common, especially among larger stockowners. Thus, the figure of 797 is in itself a significant indicator of asset concentration.

However, this is only a tip of the iceberg. Since 1974–75 there has been an increased concentration of corporate asset ownership in Malaysia, even among the top 797 stockowners. This corporate elite represents a tiny fraction of the total number of stockowners in the country who, in turn, represent a very small proportion of the total population. At the end of 1983 the total number of shares issued by the set of 145 corporations was 5,201,893,243, representing an everage of 6,526,842 share for each of the 797 shareholders. However, this is a very misleading average because of the highly skewed pattern of ownership as can be seen in Table 5.6. Just eight, the top 1 per cent of the 797 owners, accounted for 32.23 per cent of the total number of shares, whereas the bottom 50 per cent accounted for only 1.92 per cent.

Table 5.7: The Top 40 Shareholders according to Number of Shares Held

1.	Permodalan Nasional Bhd	432,988,858
2.	The Malaysian Multi-Purpose Cooperative Society Bhd	241,785,155
3.	Pemegang Amanah Saham Raya, Sekim ASN	229, 923,632
4.	Malaysian Oriental Holdings Bhd	227,923,945
5.	Batu Kawan Bhd	159,251,510
6.	Multi-Purpose Holdings Bhd	134,150,943
7.	Sime Darby Nominees S/B	132,663,590
8.	ASEAM Malaysian Nominees S/B	117,970,503
9.	Harrisons & Crosfield PLC	99,986,981
10.	KL Kepong Bhd	92,886,450
11.	Lembaga Tabung Angkatan Tentera	92,789,834
12.	FELDA	78,895,238
13.	HK & Shanghai Bank (S) Nominees P/L	66,602,199
14.	Syarikat Nominee Bumiputera S/B	63,513,788
15.	Hong Leong Co. (M) Bhd	58,103,799
16.	Tonnage Investment Lines Ltd. SA	57,177,400
17.	ABERCOM Nominees P/L	56,955,350
18.	Chelwood Trading & Investment Co. Ltd	55,440,000
19.	Bank Bumiputera Malaysia Bhd	54,000,000
20.	Cartaban (M) Nominees S/B	52,708,020
21.	DM Holdings S/B	51,000,000
22.	Lembaga Urusan & Tabung Haji	50,102,941
23.	The East Asiatic Co. Ltd., Copenhagen	48,750,000
24.	Shell Overseas Holdings	45,000,000
25.	Soo Lay Holdings S/B	45,000,000
26.	Glenealy Plantations (M) Bhd	42,941,842
27.	KKP Holdings S/B	42,000,000
28.	Chulan Nominees S/B	40,020,990
29.	Bank Simpanan Nasional	39,188,286
30.	Employees Provident Fund	38,136,927
31.	Pegi MPH S/B	36,720,000
32.	Pernas Engineering S/B	36,342,292
33.	Guinness Overseas Ltd.	36,009,000
34.	Mayban Nominees S/B	35,460,187
35.	Esso Eastern Inc.	35,100,000
36.	Syarikat Permodalan Kebangsaan Bhd	31,302,926
37.	Central Sugars Bhd	30,817,800
38.	Kuok Brothers S/B	30,091,300
39.	Parit Perak Holdings Bhd	29,938,677
40.	Komplek Kewangan Industries S/B	26,636,000

	Sub-Total	3,276,276,363
	Grand Total	5.2 billion

Source: 1983 KLSE *Annual Companies Handbook*, Vol. IX

What were the trends in the distribution of shareholdings among the top 797 owners since 1974–75? Compared to Lim's results, Table 5.6 suggests three important findings. The share of the bottom 90 per cent of 797 stockowners declined from 24.3 per cent in 1974–75 to 22.3 per cent at the end of 1983. The top 10 per cent increased their share from 75.7 per cent to 77.7 per cent. The biggest gainers were the largest eight stockowners representing the top 1 per cent — i.e. the elite of the elite — whose stockownership rose from 29.15 per cent to 32.23 per cent.

Overall, the Gini coefficient of inequality, which was already extremely high at 0.83 in 1974–75 further worsened to 0.84 in 1983.[24] By comparison, the Gini coeffient of income distribution is almost one-half,[25] implying that corporate assets are very much more unequally distributed than national income. Yet, the Malaysian distribution of income is among the worst in the world.

The Top 40 Shareholders of 1983

Table 5.7 lists, in descending order according to number of shares owned, the largest 40 shareholders of the 145 corporations covered. The National Equity Corporation (PNB), created just five years ago to manage the National Unit Trust Fund (ASN), is the largest single shareholder, accounting for 8.3 per cent of the total number of shares in the corporations covered. Another related Bumiputera corporation, Pemegang ASN, owned a further 4.6 per cent. The second largest shareholder was the MCA-dominated Malaysian Multi-Purpose Cooperative Society owning 4.6 per cent of the total and a related holding company, Multi-Purpose Holdings, owned a further 2.6 per cent. Collectively, the top 40 shareholders owned 62.98 per cent of the total number of shares.

Also noteworthy in Table 5.7 is the prominence of the Armed Forces Provident Fund, LTAT (in 11th rank), FELDA (in 12th rank) and the Pilgrims' Management and Fund Board, LUTH (in 22nd rank). FELDA was studied in Chapter 3. The next chapter will present case studies of techniques of elite enrichment by further examining PNB, LTAT and LUTH.

Nominee Stockownership

At this stage, it is enlightening to focus on another significant trend revealed by the analysis of stockownership: the increasing importance of *nominee stockowners*. At the end of 1983, 20 per cent of the top 797 stockowners were nominees. The 132 nominee stock-

Table 5.8: Nominee Stockholders by Size

Size of shares	Stockholders		Stockholding		Nominal value of stockholding	
	No.	%	Total No.	Average	Total value	Average
1. Small (1–100,000)	12	9.09	685,385	57,115	694,785	57,899
2. Medium (100,001–1,000,000)	43	32.58	22,238,573	517,176	22,281,823	518,182
3. Large (1,000,001–10,000,000)	50	37.88	157,067,930	3,141,359	151,362,081	3,027,242
4. Very Large (Over 10,000,000)	27	20.45	893,923,150	33,108,265	757,421,683	28,052,655
Total	132	100.00	1,073,915,038	8,135,720	931,760,372	7,058,791

Source: 1983 KLSE *Annual Companies Handbook*, Vol. IX

owners owned, on average, 7.1 million shares. Yet there was a wide distribution in this group as well. About 20 per cent of the nominees each owned more than 10 million shares, whereas 55 of them, or 42 per cent of the total, each owned less than 1 million shares (Table 5.8).

Nominee stockownership is a technique of concealing the identity of the owner or beneficiary. It is evident that, under the NEP equity restructuring, there has been a significant rise in the incidence of this sheltering technique. According to data from Sieh Mei Ling,[26] 11.5 per cent of total value of shareholdings in 1974–75 were owned by nominees. Our results show that, at the end of 1983, this proportion had risen to 20.4 per cent.

Conclusion

The evidence reviewed above shows that the NEP strategy of equity restructuring by trusteeship has resulted in increased wealth concentration and much of this has been financed by mobilising national savings. In fact, there has been extensive use of *forced savings* by such agencies as ASN, FELDA, EPF, SOSCO etc. The system's major loophole is that the trustees have ignored accountability, typically (as we have seen in the case of the ASN) by separating decision-making and control of funds from nominal ownership. Without adequate checks and balances, there are always temptations and opportunities for the trustees to enrich themselves, by manipulating resource allocation, through cartelisation, collusion and corruption.

Concentration of Human Capital

Education, particularly higher education, has always been valued by the Malays, Chinese and Indians as an *investment good* — often the best and the only way to achieve social and economic upward mobility.[27] The consumption-value of education is, of course, highly respected. In a multi-racial society, academic performance and qualifications have loomed uppermost in the minds and career plans of students and their parents. This, in turn, has resulted in the phenomenon of *credentialism*,[28] where undue emphasis is placed on paper qualifications by prospective employers, particularly the government. Malaysian credentialism is basically an institutionalised form of asset acquiring (i.e. a degree or diploma) which will yield a higher lifetime income. Furthermore there is intense competition for university places to acquire those assets. Typically, there is a heavy excess demand for domestic university places, spilling over into foreign universities.[29]

Under the NEP trusteeship the capital value of higher education has been greatly enhanced precisely because the trustees have created a large-scale demand for qualified Malay manpower in line with their objective of restructuring employment. In effect, they signalled to the *rakyat* that the path out of poverty and under-development was through the acquisition of human capital. The trustees, of course, retained the power of sponsoring this acquisition (through scholarships) and certifying its quality (by recognising the degrees and diplomas earned).

The first step in human capital formation under the NEP trusteeship was one of stocktaking. The 1973 Manpower Survey,[30] conducted by the Economic Planning Unit for the Third Malaysia Plan, was based on the correct assumption that there was a critical underinvestment in Malay human capital. It provided detailed occupational and educational requirements through to 1990. It called for 'a sizeable expansion in the production of scientific and technical personnel' and a 'vast expansion of personnel and facilities for education at the secondary and tertiary levels of education in the sciences and technologies'.[31]

As a result of these forecasts and expectations, there has been a rapid expansion in the Malaysian university system, with five new universities opening during 1969–80 and a fourfold increase in enrolment.[32] At the same time there has been a vast expansion in government scholarships, both at local universities and for overseas study.

What has been the consequence of this large and sudden explosion in human capital formation? Did it increase the supply of technical, scientific and professional manpower? Which groups benefited from it?

The IPT/UM Survey of 1982/83 Graduates

A comprehensive survey, covering about 50 per cent of the graduates of each of the five universities in Malaysia, was carried out during the summer of 1983 by the Institute of Advanced Studies (Institut Pengajian Tinggi—IPT) of the University of Malaya to answer these questions empirically.[33] The results showed that two out of every three students in Malaysian universities were on government scholarships. It was also revealed that nearly four of every five scholarships were awarded to Malays. The Chinese share was only 14.4 per cent, the Indian 4.3 per cent, and that of East Malaysians 2.9 per cent. Other major results were as follows:

Government as a Monopsonist. One of the most important findings of the IPT/UM survey was that government scholarships had been used almost exclusively for High-Level Manpower (HLM) development in the public sector. Thus, more than four of every five employed graduates with scholarships worked for the public sector, 67 per cent for the government and another 14.5 per cent for statutory bodies. Only 16.2 per cent worked for the private sector, and a negligible number were self-employed (Table 5.9).

Table 5.9: Employed Scholarship Holders by Sector of Employment and Race

Employer	Total Scholars		Race							
			Malays		Chinese		Indians		Others	
	No.	%	No.	%	No.	%	No.	%	No.	%
Government	530	67.0	421	70.3	66	52.8	16	45.7	27	84.4
Stat. Body	115	14.5	95	15.9	12	9.6	5	14.3	3	9.4
Private sector	128	16.2	71	11.9	42	33.6	13	37.1	2	6.2
Self-employed	5	0.6	3	0.5	2	1.6	0	0	0	0
Missing cases	13	1.6	9	1.5	3	2.4	1	2.8	0	0
Total	791	100.0	599	100.0	125	100.0	35	100.0	32	100.0

Source: IPT/UM Graduates' Survey 1983

These results strongly imply that the Malaysian government is not only the main employer of HLM, in fact it is virtually a monopsonist. Universities exist to service its staff requirements. The traditional tool of this monopsony power is bonding.

Bonding. No less than 90 per cent of the 1982/3 graduates on scholarship were under bond, obliged to work for the government for a minimum period of time upon completion of their studies, or to pay a cash indemnity. Two-thirds of the bonded graduates were committed to seven years' service, and about 10 per cent to ten years or more. The typical indemnity for discharge was $50,000–$70,000.

While bonding, a practice inherited from colonial times, represents a bargain in developing HLM for the public sector, it is particularly burdensome on lower income households. The IPT/ UM survey found that the typical scholarship cost represented only about one-third of the total (undiscounted) cost of acquiring a bachelor's degree. The remaining two-thirds was borne by the student himself, as foregone income, and by the parents. Thus, the cost-saving realised by the sponsoring agency is a higher proportion of the household income for a graduate from a lower-income household than one from a higher-income household. As a result, the job mobility of such graduates is more restricted than of graduates from well-to-do families.

Generalist-type Manpower. The surveyed graduates were classified into eight principal groups of field of study, consolidating a total of 47 specific degrees granted in the five Malaysian universities (Table 5.10). These were further subdivided into two main categories: (1) Generalist degree holders comprising degrees in Arts, Humanities and Social Sciences; General Science; and Economics and Business Administration; and (2) Professional degree holders

Table 5.10: Distribution of Scholarships by Fields and Race

Fields of study	Total		Racial shares			
	No.	%	Malays	Chinese	Indians	Others
1. Arts, Humanities and Soc. Science	388	29.7	78.9	14.2	3.6	3.3
2. General Science	430	32.9	77.2	13.2	4.7	4.9
3. Economics and Business Administration	183	14.0	77.1	15.3	6.0	1.6
4. Law	20	1.5	85.0	0	10.0	5.0
5. Health Science	48	3.7	83.3	10.4	0	6.3
6. Agricultural Sciences	89	6.8	73.0	16.9	1.1	9.0
7. Architecture, Surveying, Urban and Regional Planning	64	4.9	92.2	6.3	0	1.5
8. Engineering	84	6.4	69.1	20.2	8.3	2.4
9. Missing Cases	2	0.1				
TOTALS						
1–9	1,308	100.0				
Generalist 1–3	1,001	76.6	77.9		22.1	
Professional 4–8	305	23.3	78.4		21.6	

Source: IPT/UM Graduates' Survey, 1983

comprising graduates in Law; Health Sciences; Agricultural Sciences; Architecture, Surveying, Urban and Regional Planning; and Engineering.

The results showed that 76.6 per cent of the total 1982/3 graduates on government scholarships were Generalists, while only 23.3 per cent were in the Professional fields. Evidently, government scholarships in the Malaysian university system were not geared to the development of technical and professional manpower despite the original, planned policy objectives. In both the Generalist and Professional fields, Malay graduates on scholarship accounted for about 78 per cent of the total graduates. In Engineering the Malay share was significantly less while in Architecture, Surveying and Urban and Regional Planning it was more.

Social Overinvestment. In an earlier economic evaluation of public expenditures on Malaysian education[34] the main conclusion reached was that 'Malaysia is or soon will be overinvesting in education.' Our results confirm this prediction. In fact, under the NEP trusteeship the scale of social overinvestment and hoarding of human capital in the government sector has worsened considerably, leading to an 'oversized'[35] public sector. The estimated social rates of return for scholarship holders were less than 5 per cent (Table 5.11). By comparison, the rates payable on term deposits in commercial banks are about double.

However, human capital formation under the trusteeship system is extremely profitable in private terms. Thus, private rates of return, for those on scholarships are in the region of 15–20 per

Table 5.11: Private and Social Internal Rates of Return on Human Capital Formation in Malaysian University System, by Race and Type of Graduates

Race	Non-scholarship		Scholarship holders	
	Private IRR	Social IRR	Private IRR	Social IRR
Malay	0.122	0.076	0.173	0.040
Chinese	0.116	0.071	0.189	0.043
Indian	0.108	0.065	0.189	0.048
E. Malaysian	0.091	0.050	0.200	0.051
Others	0.096	0.056	0.189	0.048
All	0.122	0.076	0.173	0.040

Source: IPT/UM Graduates' Survey, 1983

Table 5.12: Distribution of Scholarships by Total Household Monthly Income and Race

Total Household Monthly Income[a]	Total Scholars No.	%	Population Share[b]	Malays		Chinese		Indians	
				Scholarship Share	Population Share	Scholarship Share	Population Share	Scholarship Share	Population Share
$ 0–300	153	12.3	49.4	14.2	63.2	3.4	26.0	9.5	39.7
301–500	377	30.3	22.1	32.5	19.0	20.7	26.2	26.4	29.4
501–1,000	394	31.7	18.2	30.1	12.9	41.9	27.7	39.6	20.5
1,000+	317	25.5	10.3	22.9	4.9	34.0	20.1	24.5	10.4
Missing Cases	3	0.2	–	0.3	–	–	–	–	–
Total	1,244	100.0	100.0	100.0	100.0	100.0	100.0	100.0	100.0

Notes: a. From all sources including remittances from family members, relatives, etc., farm income, dividends, interest, pension and rental income.
b. From 1977 Agriculture Census, Appendix Table 13

Source: IPT/UM Graduates' Survey, 1983

cent. Those who go on to acquire university education in Malaysia are heavily subsidised, especially those on scholarships.

Accessibility. Yet access to university education is heavily regressive, benefiting the well-to-do. According to the IPT/UM survey, government scholarships were distributed in a heavily pro-rich manner. While this was true of every race, there were significant intra-racial differences in the opportunity of a getting a scholarship (Table 5.12).

In the IPT/UM survey, poor households were defined as those having less than $300 total monthly income. The scholarship share of these poor households was only 12.3 per cent, against their population share of 49.4 per cent. The richest 10 per cent of the population accounted for about 25 per cent of the scholarship awards. Overall, these results confirmed the unequal accessibility and regressive distribution of higher educational expenditures in Malaysia.[36]

When the characteristic of race is controlled, it first appears that the distribution of scholarships is least regressive among the Malays and most regressive among the Chinese. Of the total number of scholarships awarded to Malays, 14.2 per cent went to poor Malay households, compared to 3.4 per cent awarded to the Chinese. However, after standardising for population shares, the situation is altered drastically. The intra-Malay inequality of opportunity is far greater than that of non-Malays. For every chance that a poor household has of getting a government scholarship, the richest group has 21 chances, compared to 13 and 10 chances for the richest Chinese and Indian households respectively.

Apart from being heavily pro-Malay, the method of awarding government scholarships is even more heavily biased in favour of the richer Malay households. To a lesser extent, it also favours the richer Chinese and Indian households. The scholarship policy has become a public policy tool generating inequality in income distribution and promoting an elitist concentration of human capital. In fact, such inequalities and elitist tendencies appear to be further reinforced in the case of scholarships for overseas studies which are distributed in an even more biased and elitist manner.

Conclusion. These results are contrary to the original objectives of the NEP trusteeship. Neither human nor corporate capital restructuring policies were intended as tools of wealth concentration for the exclusive benefit of elites. The objectives clearly were to promote balanced development across the Malay ethnic groups. Yet, within a relatively short space of time, trusteeship has emerged as an institutionalised system of elite enrichment. Why? It would appear that the trustees have taken advantage of their privileged status, access to information and power over the decision-making process. At the root of the problem is the separation of control from ownership, which leads to inadequate accountability on the part of the trustees — a situation which, as will be shown in the following chapter, can easily be abused.

Notes

1. J. J. Puthucheary, *Ownership and Control in the Malayan Economy*.
2. Ibid.
3. Slimming, *Malaysia: Death of a Democracy*; Vorys, *Democracy Without Consensus*.
4. Bank Negara Malaysia, *Money and Banking in Malaysia*, Kuala Lumpur, 1979, particularly Ch. 11 'Savings Institutions'.
5. For a critical analysis of the Malaysian balance of payments, see R. V. Navaratnam, 'Malaysia's Fiscal and Balance of Payment Problems', in *The Malaysian Economy at the Crossroads*, edited by Lim Lin Lean and Chee Peng Lim, pp. 105–15.
6. R. Thillainathan, 'Trends and Implications of the Malaysian Public Debt', *UMBC Review*, vol. XIX, no. 1, 1983, pp. 15–28.
7. An analysis of the Armed Forces Provident Fund is given in Ch. 6, pp. 136–8. For an analysis of the Multi-Purpose Holdings, see Ch. 6, pp. 144–7.
8. For a historical description of the EPF, see Bank Negara, *Money and Banking in Malaysia*, pp. 228–32, and the special publication: *Employees Provident Fund, 1951–1981*, EPF Kuala Lumpur (no date). On SOSCO, see Bank Negara, pp. 233–4 and *Utusan Konsumer*, Consumer Association of Penang, July 1982.
9. See the Chairman's statement in the EPF publication referred to in Note 8.
10. *Utusan Konsumer*, July 1982, p. 1.
11. *The Pilgrims Management and Fund Board*, Kuala Lumpur (no date), p. 18.
12. This information has been obtained directly from LUTH.
13. Sieh-Lee Mei Ling, 'The scheme for Bumiputera Investment in Malaysia: Some Implications' in *The Fourth Malaysia Plan, Economic Perspectives*, edited by Jomo K. Sundaram and R. J. G. Wells, Malaysian Economic Association, Kuala Lumpur, 1983, pp. 92–7.
14. PERNAS, *Annual Report 1982*, p. 43.
15. H. Peyman, 'A Dividend for the People' and 'The Great Asset Shuffle', *Far Eastern Economic Review*, January 23–29, 1981, pp. 52–4.
16. The importance of the distinction between immediate and ultimate control is discussed extensively by Sieh-Lee Mei Ling, *Ownership and Control of Malaysian Manufacturing Corporations*, University of Malaya Bookshop, Kuala Lumpur, 1984.
17. Amanah Saham Nasional Bhd, *Deed of Trust*, Kuala Lumpur, 1981, clause 36(4). For the purposes of this provision, units held or deemed to be held by the managers and PNB are disregarded in calculating the required number.

18. Toh Kin Woon, *The State in Economic Development: A Case Study of Malaysia's New Economic Policy*, PhD Thesis, University of Malaya, January 1982, p. 237.

19. Permodalan Nasional Berhad, *Annual Report 1981, p. 25 and Annual Report 1982*, p. 28.

20. 1983 KLSE *Annual Companies Handbook,* vol. IX.

21. Lim Mah Hui, *Ownership and Control of the One Hundred Largest Corporations in Malaysia*, Oxford University Press, Singapore, 1981.

22. Sieh-Lee Mei Ling, *Ownership and Control of Malaysian Manufacturing Corporations*, University of Malaya Cooperative Bookshop Ltd., Kuala Lumpur, 1983.

23. A typical practice where disclosure is avoided is to declare to the Registrar of Companies that corporate information is available from the company's secretary on application, but such application turns out to be an exercise in futility.

24. The Gini coefficient was computed using the formula at the bottom of Table 5.6. On the other hand, Lim (*Ownership and Control*, pp. 28–9 and Note 6, p. 33) used a different method. His original coefficient of 0.847 was recalculated using our method to ensure comparability.

25. Tan Tat-Wai, *Income Distribution and Determination in West Malaysia*, Oxford University Press, Kuala Lumpur, 1982; Donald R. Snodgrass, *Inequality and Economic Development in Malaysia*, Oxford University Press, Kuala Lumpur, 1980.

26. Sieh Lee Mei Ling, 'Shareholding of Non-personal Investors in Manufacturing Companies of Malaysia', *Review of Income and Wealth*, March 1980, Table 2, p. 118.

27. Chan Wang, 'Governmental Intervention in Ethnic Stratification: Effects on the Distribution of Students among Fields of Study', *Comparative Education Review*, vol. 21, no. 1, February 1977, pp. 110–23; Tham Seong Chee, 'Issues in Malaysian Education: Past, Present and Future', *Journal of Southeast Asian Studies*, vol. X, no. 2, September 1979, pp. 321–50.

28. D. Mazumdar, *The Urban Labour Market and Income Distribution in Peninsular Malaysia*, Oxford University Press, New York, 1981. For a discussion of the alternative theories of education in the Malaysian context, see Snodgrass, *Inequality and Economic Development*, especially pp. 252–60.

29. In 1980 the number of Malaysian students overseas was estimated to be 39,908, whereas in the same year enrolment in degree-level courses in Malaysian universities numbered 20,764. Source: *The Fourth Malaysian Plan*, Table 21.2, p. 349 and para. 992, p. 350.

30. *The Report of the Manpower Survey in Malaysia 1973*, Kuala Lumpur (no date).

31. Ibid., para. 264, pp. 91–2.

32. Yip Yat Hoong, 'The Cost of University Education in Malaysia', *RIHED Bulletin*, vol. 10, no. 1, January–March 1983, Table II, p. 25.

33. The full details and results are in the forthcoming report by Ozay Mehmet and Yip Yat Hoong, *Human Capital Formation in Malaysian Universities. A Socioeconomic Profile of the 1983 Graduates*, IPT, University of Malaya, 1985.

34. O. E. Hoerr, 'Education, Income and Equity in Malaysia', *Economic Development and Cultural Change*, vol. 21, no. 2, January 1973, pp. 247–73.

35. The Deputy Prime Minister, Musa Hitam stated that 'the public service employs 1.2 million people which is 23 per cent of the total national work force of 5.2 million.' See 'Too many public servants for our own good: Musa. Trimming all that "fat"', *Malaysia New Sunday Times*, 11 March 1984.

36. J. Meerman, *Public Expenditure in Malaysia: Who Benefits and Why?*, Oxford University Press, New York, 1979.

Appendix

Table 5A.1: The 145 Companies Used in the Analysis

Name of Company	Paid-up Capital
*COMPANY TYPE: INDUSTRIAL	
Allied Malayan Development Bhd	8250000
Amalgamated Properties & Industries Bhd	73693333
Amalgamated Steel Mills Bhd	85000000
Bata (Malaysia) Bhd	20000000
Berjaya Kawat Bhd	14270000
Boustead Holdings Bhd	71312503
Carlsberg Brewery Malaysia Bhd	30600000
Central Sugars Bhd	24033332
Chemical Company of Malaysia Bhd	30000000
Chocolate Products (Malaysia) Bhd	11000000
Datuk Kermat Holdings Bhd	15000000
Dragon & Phoenix Bhd	26493000
Dunlop Malaysia Industries Bhd	100000000
Duta Consolidated Bhd	27035000
Dutch Baby Milk Industries (Malaysia) Bhd	8000000
The East Asiatic Company (Malaysia) Bhd	75000000
Electrical & Allied Industries Bhd	3120000
Esso Malaysia Bhd	54000000
Federal Cables, Wires & Metal Manufacturing Bhd	23416000
Federal Flour Mills Bhd	85000000
Fima Metal Box Bhd	20645816
FOLEX Industries Bhd	5400000
Fusan Fishing Net Manufacturing Bhd	7940625
General Corporation Bhd	60766008
General Lumber Holdings Bhd	36348000
The George Town Dispensary Bhd	402327
Guinness Malaysia Bhd	72000000
Gula Perak Bhd	3400000
Hume Industries (Malaysia) Bhd	113894191
Industrial Oxygen Incorporation Bhd	8500000
Jack Chia Enterprises (Malaysia) Bhd	25256000
Keck Seng (Malaysia) Bhd	56000000
Khong Guan Holdings Malaysia Bhd	23616000
Kuala Lumpur Industries Bhd	10000000
Lien Hoe Industries Bhd	10328906
Lion Corporation Bhd	12000000
Magnum Corporation Bhd	111339342
Malayan Cables Bhd	12900000
Malayan Flour Mills Bhd	30000000
Malayan Glass Factory Bhd	18900000
Malayan United Industries Bhd	341176875
Malayawata Steel Bhd	67194567

Table 5A.1 — *continued*

Name of Company	Paid-up Capital
Malaysian Mosaics Bhd	3000000
Malaysian Oxygen Bhd	30758334
Malaysian Resources Corporation Bhd	55344000
Malaysian Tobacco Company Bhd	105300000
Malex Industries Bhd	13300000
Menang Corporation (Malaya) Bhd	99000000
Multi-Purpose Holdings Bhd	450616949
MWE Holdings Bhd	8700000
The New Straits Times Press (Malaysia) Bhd	22958334
Norsechem (Malaya) Bhd	6600000
Pacific Chemicals Bhd	2080000
Palmco Holdings Bhd	88350000
Pan Malaysia Cement Works Bhd	65775000
Pan Malaysia Rubber Industries Bhd	25000000
Paper Products (Malaya) Bhd	22666667
Paramount Corporation Bhd	61837713
Promet Bhd	207300000
Public Corporation Bhd	10370466
Raleigh Cycles (Malaysia) Bhd	16125000
Roxy Electric Industries (Malaysia) Bhd	18816000
Sanyo Industries (Malaysia) Bhhd	3000000
Shell Refining Company (FOM) Bhd	60000000
Sin Heng Chan (Malaya) Bhd	18359375
South East Asia Lumber Corporation Bhd	18200000
South Johore Amalgamated Holdings Bhd	5750000
South Malaysia Industries Bhd	8100000
SPK-Sentosa Corporation Bhd	10083333
Supreme Corporation Bhd	242558160
Supreme Plantations Industries Bhd	30823462
Taiping Textiles Bhd	65075000
Tasek Cement Bhd	111820000
TDM Bhd	19607072
Textile Corporation of Malaya Bhd	14850000
Timuran Holdings Bhd	10000000
Toshiba (Malaysia) Bhd	5000000
Tractors Malaysia Holdings Bhd	108000000
The Tropical Veneer Company Bhd	11000000
UAC Bhd	52600000
Ulu Benut Consolidated Industries (M) Bhd	7116615
Unilite Electrical Industries Bhd	5400000
Universal Cable (M) Bhd	35000000
Yeo Hiap Seng (Malaysia) Bhd	43700000
Subtotal	4033423305

Table 5A.1 — *continued*

Name of Company	Paid-up Capital
*COMPANY TYPE: FINANCE	
Malayan Banking Bhd	180000000
Malaysia Building Society Bhd	76628291
Malaysian American Assurance Company Bhd	4000000
Public Bank Bhd	70000000
Subtotal	330628291
*COMPANY TYPE: HOTEL	
Faber Merlin Malaysia Bhd	131815275
Subtotal	131815275
*COMPANY TYPE: PROPERTY	
Bandar Raya Developments Bhd	261293179
Bolton Properties Bhd	43282040
Ipoh Garden Bhd	67500000
Island and Peninsular Development Bhd	35942400
San Holdings Bhd	16000000
United Estates Projects Bhd	75000000
Subtotal	499017619
*COMPANY TYPE: OIL-PALM	
Austral Enterprises Bhd	15000000
Batu Kawan Bhd	118500000
Benta Plantation Bhd	14000000
Consolidated Plantations Bhd	232323073
Harrisons Malaysia Plantations Bhd	333905346
Kemayan Oil Palm Bhd	25000000
Negri Sembilan Oil Palm Bhd	29172710
United Plantations Bhd	99500000
Subtotal	867401129
*COMPANY TYPE: TIN	
Adkam Tin Bhd	14000000
Austral Amalgamated Tin Bhd	10000000
Ayer Hitam Dredging Malaysia Bhd	6100000
Berjuntai Tin Dredging Bhd	30526200
Kampung Lanjut Tin Dredging Bhd	6000000
Kamunting Tin Dredging (M) Bhd	2006250
Kramat Tin Dredging Bhd	3960000

Table 5A.1 — *continued*

Name of Company	Paid-up Capital
Kuala Lumpur Tin Fields Bhd	3690000
Kuchai Development Bhd	1311995
Malaysia Mining Corporation Bhd	41172579
Petaling Tin Bhd	7058944
Rahman Hydraulic Tin Bhd	22500000
The Sungei Besi Mines Malaysia Bhd	3412950
Talam Mines Bhd	1890000
Timah Langat Bhd	8554500
Tongkah Harbour Tin Dredging Bhd	4420000
Tronoh Mines Malaysia Bhd	10315785
Subtotal	176919203
*COMPANY TYPE: RUBBER	
The Ayer Hitam Planting Syndicate Bhd	2268275
The Ayer Molek Rubber Company Bhd	1200000
Batu Lintang Rubber Company	17723130
Bedford Plantations Bhd	2550000
The Bukit Katil Rubber Estates Bhd	3150000
Chin Teck Plantations Bhd	14850000
Duff Development Bhd	13956360
Dunlop Estates Bhd	72000000
Gadek (Malaysia) Bhd	8605587
Glenealy Plantations (M) Bhd	42651264
Highlands and Lowlands Bhd	151083914
Jeram Kuantan (M) Bhd	1726510
Kluang Rubber Company (M) Bhd	2006385
Kuala Lumpur Kepong Bhd	335000752
Kundong Tanjung Pau Company Bhd	3802500
Malakoff Bhd	42744320
Malaysian Plantations Bhd	60000000
Mentakab Rubber Company (M) Bhd	1400674
The New Serendah Rubber Company Bhd	24592192
Parit Perak Holdings Bhd	3000000
Premium Holdings Bhd	11805000
Riverview Rubber Estates Bhd	10808408
Sungei Bagan Rubber Company (M) Bhd	1890361
Taiping Consolidated Bhd	2000000
The Temerloh Rubber Estates Bhd	15383760
Subtotal	846199392
Total	6885404214

Table 5A.2: Companies with no Information on Shareholders

Name of Company	Paid-up Capital $
*COMPANY TYPE: INDUSTRIAL	
Ajinomoto (Malaysia) Bhd	23354240
Aluminium Company of Malaysia Bhd	48937500
Cold Storage (Malaysia) Bhd	25000000
Cycle and Carriage Bintang Bhd	59500000
Ganda Holdings Bhd	23742198
Genting Bhd	217396367
George Kent (Malaysia) Bhd	9000000
Gold Coin (Malaysia) Bhd	15000000
Hong Leong Industries Bhd	61397000
India-Malaysia Textiles Bhd	1558225
J & P Coats (Malaysia) Bhd	3675000
Johan Holdings Bhd	34170321
Loytape Bhd	3500000
Malayan Cement Bhhd	54435798
Malaysia Textiles Industries Bhd	29979025
Malaysian Containers (1974) Bhd	8925000
Matshutita Electric Company (M) Bhd	19687500
The North Borneo Timbers Bhd	60060000
Oriental Holdings Bhd	83500000
Pegi Malaysia Bhd	49112538
Perlis Plantations Bhd	127767000
Rothmans of Pall Mall (M) Bhd	68850000
Setron (Malaysia) Bhd	37700000
Sime Darby Bhd	391689328
South Pacific Textile Industries Bhd	25904750
Synthetic Resins (M) Bhd	28491746
Tan Chong Motor Holdings Bhd	96000000
United Engineers (Malaysia) Bhd	50000000
United Malayan Flour Mills Bhd	6000000
United Motor Works (M) Holdings Bhd	145068917
The Wilkinson Process Rubber Company Bhd	12385756
Worldwide Holdings Bhd	4000000
Subtotal	1825788209
*COMPANY TYPE: FINANCE	
Hong Leong Credit Bhd	43800600
MBF Holdings Bhd	30700000
South East Asia Development Corporation Bhd	7000000
Subtotal	81500600

Table 5A.2 — *continued*

Name of Company	Paid-up Capital
*COMPANY TYPE: HOTEL	
Rasa Sayang Beach Hotels (Penang) Bhd	65000000
Subtotal	65000000
*COMPANY TYPE: PROPERTY	
Petaling Gardens Bhd	83363500
San Holdings Bhd	16000000
Selangor Properties Bhd	96291665
Subtotal	195655165
*COMPANY TYPE: OIL-PALM	
Lingui Development Bhd	9790908
Selangor Coconuts Bhd	58523540
Subtotal	68314448
COMPANY TYPE: TIN	
Kesang Holdings Bhd	23599946
Killinghall Tin (M) Bhd	10000000
Larut Tin Fields Bhd	12924000
Selangor Dredging Bhd	19580993
Subtotal	66104939
*COMPANY TYPE: RUBBER	
Asiatic Development Bhd	90000000
Guthrie Ropel Bhd	82352941
The Kuala Sidim Rubber Company Bhd	22194676
Kulim (M) Bhd	41427246
The United Malacca Rubber Estates Bhd	13325163
Subtotal	239300026
Total	2541663387

6 THE SOCIAL COSTS OF TRUSTEESHIP: DEFICITS, 'DISTRIBUTIONAL COALITIONS' AND QUASI-RENTS

Introduction

In Chapter 1 the NEP trusteeship was described as an *infant industry* conceived for the collective benefit of the Malay community, which historically manifested a high incidence of poverty. In subsequent chapters we reviewed the poverty impact of the various policies initiated under the NEP. One of the major conclusions emerging from the review is that the NEP trusteeship system is subject to the inherent weaknesses of the infant industries: viz. (1) that the 'infant may never grow up' and (2) that it may skew income and wealth distribution in favour of non-competing groups who derive quasi-rents and other forms of unearned rewards from their influential and privileged status. More specifically and in particular reference to the second point, the trusteeship system may be enriching the trustees at the expense of the nominal beneficiaries.

In this chapter attention will be focused on the social costs of trusteeship. Why do these costs arise? How do non-competing groups get rewarded? What techniques of self-enrichment do they use? The chapter is organised in four parts. Part II will document the growth of state enterprise deficits, created to implement the Malaysian trusteeship. Part III will examine, with the aid of illustrative case studies, how sub-elites peddle influence and use other non-competitive means to derive quasi-rents. The final part will analyse the emerging pattern of income distribution in the light of these conclusions.

The Rising Costs of Public Enterprise

As was seen in Chapter 1, the system of NEP trusteeship led to a rapid growth and expansion of public enterprises, statutory bodies, financial institutions and trust agencies set up to implement the objectives of restructuring policy. According to one recent count[1] by the end of the first decade of the NEP, there were 91 federal public enterprises and statutory bodies plus an additional 56 state statutory bodies. Many of these are Off-Budget Agencies (OBAs), reflecting the fact they are financed outside the regular government budget and thus are not within the Auditor-General's jurisdiction.[2]

Yet all of these institutions were financed by government contributions and many still depend on public subsidies. Their growth and expansion increase the weight of state capitalism in the Malaysian economy. Most significantly, their operating losses, whether due to managerial inefficiency[3] or misallocation of funds,[4] are ultimately a drain on the productive resources of the economy. Collectively, they provide a bureaucratic maze for rent-seeking groups and networks[5] which will be discussed in the next section.

Tables 6.1 and 6.2 present data documenting the dramatic growth of state capitalism under the Malaysian trusteeship system since 1970. Total public sector expenditure in that year accounted for 28.7 per cent of GNP at market prices — an already high figure. By 1979, it represented 40 per cent, and just three years later the proportion had leapt to 61.2 per cent. Even more disturbingly, the consolidated public sector deficit, which was only 3.5 per cent of GNP in 1970, rose gradually to 8.8 per cent by 1979 and then jumped to 26.3 per cent by 1982. This last figure is one of the highest deficit/GNP ratios in the world.[6]

Table 6.1: Trends in Consolidated Public Sector Finance, 1970–1982 (Amounts in billions of $)

	1970	1979	1982
1. Consolidated public sector:			
Operating expenditures	2.4	11.4	19.2
Development expenditures	0.9	5.7	16.2
Total public sector expenditure	3.3	17.1	35.4
2. Overall deficit	0.4	3.8	15.2
3. GNP at current market prices	11.5	43.1	57.8
4. Total public sector expenditure as % of GNP	28.7	40.0	61.2
5. Consolidated public sector deficit as % of GNP	3.5	8.8	26.3

Source: Ministry of Finance, Malaysia, *Economic Report* (several issues)

Table 6.2: Outstanding Loans by the Federal Government to Certain Statutory Bodies, Companies, State Governments and Others, 1970–82 (Amounts in millions of $)

	1970	1982
1. Statutory Bodies		
Federal Land Development Authority	266	2,548
Majlis Amanah Rakyat	30	440
Urban Development Authority	–	903
National Padi and Rice Authority	–	138
2. Companies		
PERNAS	5	441
Malaysian Industrial Development Finance	38	78
Malaysian International Shipping Corporation	12	444
Malaysian Shipyard and Engineering Sdn Bhd	–	131
3. State Governments	302	3,620
4. Housing Loans to Government Officers	–	1,953
Total	653	10,696

Source: Ministry of Finance, Malaysia, *Economic Report* (several issues)

One of the most important factors contributing to these alarming deficit trends under the trusteeship system is the rapid increase of budgetary resource flows to public enterprises, statutory bodies and Bumiputera companies. This is demonstrated in Table 6.2, which contains statistics regarding outstanding loans by the federal government to four statutory bodies (viz. FELDA, MARA, UDA, and NPRA) four Bumiputera companies (viz. PERNAS, MIDF, MISC, and MSESB) and loans to state governments and housing loans to government officers. This information is far from comprehensive. Government investments in public enterprises (which stood at $2.335 billion in 1982) are excluded, as is equity participation in Bumiputera banks and financial institutions and public joint ventures. Despite its partial coverage, the data in Table 6.2 show that there has been a sharp increase in the ratio of outstanding federal loans to total public sector expenditures during 1970–82. In 1970 this ratio was 19.8 per cent. By 1982 it had risen to 30.2 per cent. (In fact, it was 36.7 per cent if federal government investments of $2.335 billion are included).

By the early 1980s it was evident that a significant number of these public enterprises and statutory bodies were incurring heavy losses and a number had already been closed down. According to data tabulated by Mavis Puthucheary,[7] the accumulated losses of 18 SEDC companies amounted to $162.9 million in 1980. Up to 1979 ten MARDEC companies had cumulative losses amounting to $67.6 million while Syarikat Jangka lost $37.1 million. All three subsidiaries of MISC had gone into liquidation in October 1980. More recently, according to the Ministry of Public Enterprises,[8] of the 314 SEDC companies, 103 had made aggregate profits of $346.8 million, while 125 had combined losses of $360.6 million. The other 86 companies did not even submit a report. In the case of financially successful companies such as PETRONAS, large amounts of funds have been exported to London banks and elsewhere to earn interest rather than being diverted into productive, development expenditures at home.

The sharp increase in the level of public resource flows to statutory bodies and public enterprises under the trusteeship system is also due in part to the economic recession after 1980. The downward rigidity of these resource flows, even during a period of austerity, is an excellent demonstration of the heavy social costs of permanent and institutionalised protectionism. Agencies dependent upon government subsidies operate as if they are insulated from business cycles. In such agencies, performance and success tend to be determined not only on the basis of productivity and efficiency but on non-competitive, bureaucratic criteria. These criteria are subject to manipulation by the rich and powerful seeking quasi-rents and other forms of unearned economic rewards. These techniques of rent-seeking behaviour will now be examined.

'Distributional Coalitions' and Rent-seeking Behaviour

An inherent characteristic of economic trusteeship is that income shares are not determined competitively. Income distribution is biased by what Mancur Olson has called 'distributional coalitions'.[9]

What are these distributional coalitions? How do they operate? They are small, powerful and influential groups, organised as cartels, seeking rewards through collusion, transaction costs and other forms of non-competitive bargains. Special interest groups, lobbies and networks are visible examples of distributional coalitions. Their paramount logic is to strike mutually enriching deals through exchange of vital information about contracts, investment opportunities, capital gains, etc. Access to such information is a closely guarded secret, monopolised by the cartel-like networks. It is a by-product of official status enjoyed by trustees who can thus utilise status as well as information for self-enriching rewards.

Non-competitive rewards derived from cartelisation occur as quasi-rents — i.e. unearned income. They skew income and wealth distribution in favour of these groups while simultaneously perpetuating mass poverty. Specifically, factors of production whose owners lack political and economic power get under-remunerated: biased management of resource allocation leads to economic exploitation.

We shall now examine, with illustrative cases, how Malaysian distributional coalitions have cornered the New Economic Policy to derive quasi-rents under the NEP trusteeship system. We shall focus on five particular distributional coalitions: (1) military, (2) religious, (3) aristocratic, (4) bureaucratic, and (5) political.

Two important qualifications should be stated at the outset. First, memberships in these coalitions often overlap as a result of kinship, professional and business ties. For example, between the top political and the top military leadership there is a tradition of close relationship fostered by intermarriage,[10] while the dividing line between senior levels of bureaucracy and political life is so thin as to be indistinguishable. There is also such a close corporate alliance between the religious and the banking elites, most evidently through interlocking directorships, that the religious coalition could also be identified as part of a larger banking cartel.

Secondly, the aim here is not to offer a taxonomy of the Malaysian elite as a sociological phenomenon but to analyse its strategy of self-enrichment through equity restructuring. In other words the concern is not with the social origins and membership characteristics of these elite subsets.[11] Rather it is to examine the ways and means by which they exercise privilege and status to bias economic decision-making for the concentration of wealth and income.

The Military Coalition: The Ericsson Telecommunications Partnership

The basis of the economic power of the military distributional coalition is its control of the Armed Forces Provident Fund — the Lembaga Tabung Angkatan Tentera (LTAT) and the Armed

Forces Cooperative. The Malaysian military brass has historically had a very close relationship with the political leadership but more recently, an increasing number of retired generals have joined the boards of companies.[12] Since 1970 the military coalition has taken advantage of the equity restructuring opportunities under the NEP to channel its large LTAT fund into profitable investments, emerging as one of the largest capitalist groups in the country. At the beginning of 1983 it ranked as the 11th largest stockowner of the 145 largest public companies listed on the Kuala Lumpur Stock Exchange covered in our survey, with equity participation in 17 such companies. Its investment portfolio was highly diversified, covering listed and nonlisted private companies. It had equity interests in plantation companies (e.g. Boustead Holdings), banking institutions (e.g. a majority stake in Habib Perwira Bank), news media, hotels and property development (e.g. Fleet), electrical products and mass communications equipment (e.g. Fleet and Perwira Ericsson).

As with other distributional coalitions, the military, controlling the expanding LTAT corporate interests, derive quasi-rents through (1) patronage and (2) non-competitive awards of government contracts. Appointments to chairmanships and directorships in the LTAT corporate structure go to close family members or are rewarded to senior military officers. For example, the chairman of the Fund is the current Secretary-General of the Ministry of Defence. The former Secretary-General of the Ministry of Defence, upon retirement, joined the Board of Directors of Boustead in which LTAT has a 34 per cent controlling share, followed by FELDA which has a 25 per cent share.[13] The brother of the chairman of the board of Habib Perwira Bank, a joint venture between LTAT and Pakistani interests, is the chairman of Fleet in which LTAT has an interest and recently entered into a joint venture with Phillips of the Netherlands.[14] FELDA has a 25 per cent equity interest in Boustead: FELDA's chairman is also the chairman of Boustead.

A recent example of a non-competitive contract award won by the LTAT military elite is the case of its joint-venture partnership with the Swedish company, Ericsson Telecommunications. The company, which has obtained 'pioneer status', qualifies for a number of tax and investment concessions, and has a plant in the Shah Alam industrial estate in Selangor employing about 150 employees, almost entirely Malay, producing electrical and mass communications products. Its joint-venture partnership with the LTAT military elite is organised on the basis of two corporations. On the one hand, there is Ericsson Telecommunications Sdn Bhd in which effective corporate control rests with the parent company which owns 70 per cent of the equity, while the LTAT interests own the remaining 30 per cent. On the other hand, there is a second holding company, called Perwira Ericsson, the equity of which is split 60:40 in favour of LTAT. Recently, Perwira Ericsson, along with NEC PERNAS, was non-competitively awarded a multi-million dollar contract for expanding and modernising the Malaysian telephone system.

The Religious Coalition: the Nestlé Restructuring Case

The rent-seeking behaviour of the distributional coalition associated with Lembaga Urusan dan Tabung Haji (LUTH) will now be examined. Analysed in the previous chapter, it is a highly successful institution in mobilising the savings of the intensely religious Malay rural communities. Thanks to these savings, LUTH has achieved rapid corporate growth under the system of NEP trusteeship. It was ranked the 22nd largest stockholder in our survey, with equity participation in 27 companies listed on the KLSE. Recently, it was allocated a controlling equity interest in Nestlé's Malaysian operations resulting in a non-competitive award of Nestlé stock on the basis of privileged connections.

The Nestlé SA of Switzerland has been in Malaysia since the early 1900s, initially as a distributor but now as an integrated manufacturer of food products with four subsidiaries and one associated company (Figure 6.1). The associate company, Malaysia Cocoa Manufacturing Sdn Bhd is a joint venture with FELDA in which FELDA has a 51 per cent share.[15] The four subsidiaries have had small levels of local participation, particularly Bumiputera and, as a result, have been obliged to restructure their equity ownership in accordance with the NEP formula of 30-30-40.

The bureaucratic procedures through which equity restructuring is approved for implementation are complex and provide an ideal opportunity for transaction costs and quasi-rents. There are at least three separate agencies involved in the approval process: the Bumiputera Participation Unit of the Ministry of Trade and Industry, the Foreign Investment Committee of the Prime Minister's Department and the Capital Issues Committee of the Bank Negara. These agencies do not have exclusive areas of

Figure 6.1: The Nestlé Restructuring Case

BEFORE RESTRUCTURING

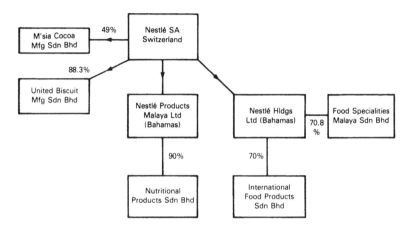

AFTER RESTRUCTURING

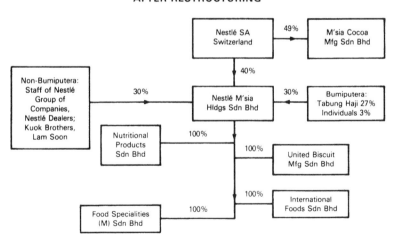

Source: *Malaysia New Straits Times*, 23 September 1983

jurisdiction, thus affording alternative points of intervention by rent-seeking elites. In theory, the first agency is intended to promote Bumiputera equity participation, the second to formulate policies for regulating and monitoring acquisitions, mergers and take-overs involving foreign firms, while the third has a supervisory role in the approval of the prospectuses of new ventures and the issuance of new shares by existing companies.

In practice, allocations of shares and stocks of restructured companies are determined primarily on a preferential basis in which influence and status are the principal criteria. The preferred beneficiaries receive quotas of equity, at discounted prices, and the size of the quota depends on the status and influence of the beneficiary. Under this system, a speculator can realise immediate significant capital gains, unlike the small investor in the ASN.

In the case of Nestlé restructuring, a new holding company was incorporated, called Nestlé Malaysia Holdings Sdn Bhd. Of the 30 per cent Bumiputera share, 27 per cent was allocated to LUTH and to one individual, the wife of the former Deputy Prime Minister and Minister of Home Affairs, Tun Dr Ismail. He and Tun Razak qualify as the founding-fathers of the NEP. Along with these Bumiputera beneficiaries of the Nestlé equity restructuring are the Chinese interests who have been Nestlé partners in the past and are now able to enlarge their stake to 30 per cent, and the company's 4,000 or so employees.[16]

Aristocratic Coalitions: The ANTAH Group of Companies

There is a large aristocratic superstructure in Malaysia clustered around the sultans who are the hereditary rulers of the states in the Federation of Malaysia, and who, under the constitution, select one of their own every five years, to act as the King of Malaysia.[17] In addition to inherited princely titles, the sultans customarily award a wide range of life peerages which are eagerly sought by status-seeking aspirants in public and business life. Such titles are more than status symbols. They can be tapped for personal enrichment. Titled personages are valued as potential members of their boards of directors or business partners by local as well as foreign firms. This practice has had two important advantages: firstly, it satisfies tokenism under the NEP requiring that Bumiputeras should be employed at all occupational levels and, secondly, it provides opportunities for quasi-rents and non-competitive rewards to win contracts, approvals and permits, or simply to clear political and bureaucratic hurdles which are regularly encountered in this environment.

In this context, it is not surprising that members of the Malaysian aristocratic elite have emerged as some of the principal rent-seekers and biggest gainers under the system of NEP trusteeship. Members of the aristocracy have derived large benefits from royalties on timber concessions, land and property development (even a gambling casino), industrial and commercial joint ventures with foreign investors, and through preferential equity participation, sometimes disguised behind nominee companies.[18]

The manner in which one particular aristocratic subset has utilised its privileged status to derive quasi-rents under the favourable conditions of the NEP will now be examined. This is the case of ANTAH Holdings Sdn Bhd, associated with the Negri Sembilan royalty. It was established in 1977 as a joint venture between Syarikat Pesaka Antah — an investment company owned by the royal family of Negri Sembilan — and the Malaysian subsidiary of Jardine, Matheson & Co., Ltd of Hong Kong. The latter provided the necessary capital to finance the venture, although on paper the equity was split 54:46 in favour of Antah. The top corporate positions were reserved for members of the Negri Sembilan royalty. The eldest son of the ruler of Negri Sembilan became chairman of the board while a brother became managing director and a sister was made a director. However, the real executive and technical functions were in the hands of expatriate directors and professional staff assigned by Jardine.[19]

The joint venture's corporate structure was skilfully crafted to take maximum advantage of opportunities in profitable influence-peddling. A total of 23 different companies were created in the areas of marketing and trading, financial services, advertising and security services, property development and offshore drilling.[20] Typically these were small companies, with paid-up capital under $500,000. Several (e.g. the offshore drilling and property development companies) never became operational. Many marginal companies were established hoping to obtain government contracts in as many areas as possible, through collusion and privileged access to contracts and information. In some cases (e.g. security guards' service and equipment leasing) this was successfully done. In others, it failed to materialise, owing to more effective lobbying from other distributional coalitions, (e.g. in the case of a telephone directory contract), owing to external factors (e.g. when declining oil prices forced multinational offshore drilling companies to lose interest) or simply due to managerial incompetence (e.g. the loss of advertising accounts). At the end of 1983 Antah Holdings decided to go public with a projected issue of shares on the Kuala Lumpur Stock Exchange.[21] The viability of the joint venture is far from certain owing to political developments in Hong Kong affecting Jardine, Matheson & Co. Ltd.[22]

The New Bureaucratic Coalitions: The National Equity Corporation

The new bureaucratic distributional coalitions created to manage equity restructuring under the NEP trusteeship will now be examined. The focus will be on the National Equity Corporation (Permodalan Nasional Berhard — PNB) which, although barely five years old, is the largest single stockowner of the 145 top companies listed on the Kuala Lumpur Stock Exchange, owning 8.3 per cent of 5.2 billion shares in these companies (Table 5.7).

The conception and evolution of the PNB represents the most direct impact of the policy of equity restructuring by accumulating corporate assets under the formula of NEP trusteeship. It has given rise to a new layer of the managerial bureaucracy which it is benefiting not only in terms of jobs and status but also from its access to potentially enriching sources of information about stock deals, and forthcoming restructuring cases.

The meteoric rise of the PNB has been made possible by the channelling of large amounts of public funds for this purpose. It is therefore not surprising that the growth of PNB investments has been so phenomenal. In 1979 the value of these investments stood at $123.5 million. By the end of 1982 PNB's investments had multiplied more than 25 times to $3.154 billion.[23] The PNB portfolio included 15 listed companies on the KLSE covered in our sample of the top 145 companies.

Such a large concentration of corporate assets, acquired so rapidly, confers tremendous powers on the bureaucratic and political elites managing portfolios and investment policy. It raises major questions of efficiency and accountability. Who are these managers? What implementation strategy do they use? How accountable are they?

The Chairman of PNB's board is the former Governor of Bank Negara, and he is also the Chairman of the ASN's board. The PNB board also includes the former chief of Armed Forces Staff, the chairman of the government-owned Malayan Banking Corporation, along with the Secretary-General of the Ministry of Trade and Industry and the Governor of Bank Negara. This particular composition is noteworthy because it interlinks the bureaucratic/ political elites with the military and the aristocratic elites on the one hand, and with the Central Bank (i.e. the source of liquidity from such agencies as EPF and SOSCO), and the Ministry of Trade and Industry (i.e the agency assigned the task of implementing the restructuring policy) on the other. Thus, under its enabling legislation, PNB is entitled to an allocation of at least 10 per cent of new shares or offers of shares, through the Ministry of Trade and Commerce.[24]

The main strategy behind PNB's investment policy has been acquisition and takeover of existing companies. At the end of 1982, over 80 per cent of its investments were in subsidiaries, including the wholly-owned Guthrie Corporation — one of the largest plantation companies in the country, formerly owned by British interests — and associated companies.[25] These acquisitions, as in other Bumiputera holding companies, have provided the PNB management team with multiple directorships on the boards of subsidiaries and associated companies. Thus, the PNB chairman is also the chairman of the Harrison Malaysian Plantations Berhad, in which PNB has a 58.5 per cent controlling interest. Another PNB director is also a Harrison board member. The former General Manager of PNB is the chairman of Malaysia Mining Corporation Berhad in which PNB has a 38 per cent interest.

Accountability is the weakest link in the PNB chain. Take, for example, rules relating to capital gains. Speculative capital gains, all tax exempt, are common on the Kuala Lumpur Stock Exchange. The KLSE is a relatively small stock exchange and any intervention by the PNB, because of its size, can influence prices of stocks and shares. Individuals privy to these interventions can realise huge capital gains. In the policy guidelines there are no conflict-of-interest provisions, nor any procedures to prevent collusion among distributional coalitions. The guidelines merely require PNB to refrain from speculative interventions.

Insider trading and speculative manipulations are not an uncommon occurrence on the KLSE and the KL Commodity Exchange (KLCE). A recent example of speculative stock manipulations on the KLCE occurred in early 1984, when a single speculator forced the price of an oil palm futures contract from less than $1,000 a ton to almost $3,000 within a matter of weeks. Once insider trading was uncovered, the price fell equally rapidly and transactions valued at $30 million were invalidated, future trading suspended and serious doubts cast about the credibility of the KLCE.[26] Subsequently, this matter was resolved by approving the speculators' large gains. In the meantime, the retail price of cooking oil went up significantly. The irony is that while capital gains are tax-exempt in Malaysia, staples such as cooking oil are subject to regressive indirect taxes. Thus, the burden of huge capital gains which enrich distributional coalitions are passed on to the lower-income households.

Political Coalitions: The UMBC-MPHB Affair

The NEP trusteeship has given rise to clusters of distributional coalitions centred on political parties or leading politicians owning and controlling corporate assets. Thus, there are UMNO-owned and controlled companies, there are MCA companies and MIC corporate interests. The ultimate control and management of these corporate interests rests with the political elites. In this section, a recent case of inter-ethnic conflict over corporate spoils — the so-called UMBC-MPHB affair — involving the UMNO and MCA political elites will be examined. Of particular interest is the fact that the opportunity for wealth concentration through equity restructuring under the NEP is by no means restricted to the Malay elites. It is also available to the wealthy and powerful in the other ethnic groups as well. In fact, as the UMBC-MPHB affair shows, the NEP has given a new impetus to inter-ethnic political bargains for mutually enriching schemes of wealth concentration.

The Multi-Purpose Holding Bhd (MPHB) is a widely-diversified conglomerate.[27] It is controlled by the Chinese business elite identified with the Malaysian Chinese Association (MCA), the second senior partner in the ruling Nasional Barisan party after the United Malay National Organisation (UMNO), along with the Malaysian Indian Congress (MIC). The MPHB was incorporated in 1975 with the objective of protecting the Chinese business interests under the new rules of equity restructuring introduced by the NEP. By 1983 it had become the largest single company in the country, measured by the size of paid-up capital, and it had no less than 13 directly-owned subsidiaries and associated companies (Figure 6.2).

The main strategy behind MPHB's meteoric growth has been its

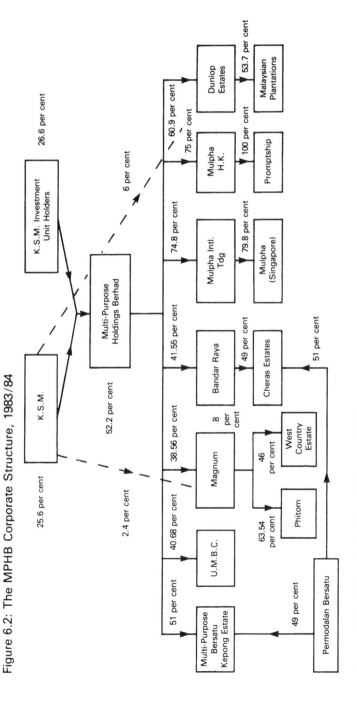

Figure 6.2: The MPHB Corporate Structure, 1983/84

Source: *Malaysia New Straits Times*, 10 February 1984.

policy of acquiring potentially profitable companies which were not realising their full potential due to poor management.[28] This strategy of carefully-staged acquisitions required a constant access to large pools of cash. So, early in 1981, MPHB launched a bid to acquire a controlling interest in the country's third-largest bank, the United Malayan Banking Corporation (UMBC). However the bid met strong initial opposition from the powerful youth wing of UMNO, whose leader argued that the deal could undermine the objectives of the NEP by placing UMBC under the effective control of the MCA. In particular, the deal would mean that the national holding company, PERNAS, would lose its control of UMBC. As a result a major inter-ethnic political conflict appeared in the offing, threatening harmony within the ruling Barisan Nasional party.[29] However, in the end, the issue was settled quietly by the top political leadership in UMNO and MCA in a manner which maximised the common corporate interests of the parties involved. Both the MPHB and PERNAS were allowed to acquire 40 per cent of the UMBC equity, on the theory that neither could then exercise a controlling interest.

The importance of the UMBC-MPHB affair lies in its demonstration of the convergence of corporate interests at the top of the inter-ethnic political structure. Ultimately, effective control and management of the Malaysian economic and financial system, as its political system, reflects an inter-ethnic elite partnership in which the Malay component is dominant. Every ethnic component is able, in varying degrees, to exercise collusion and strike profitable bargains while settling inter-ethnic political and corporate disputes. As MPHB's subsequent growth performance demonstrates, that it only acquired 40 per cent and not 51 per cent control of UMBC was of secondary importance to the paramount business strategy of securing a source of liquidity to finance its acquisitions and takeovers.

The UMBC-MPHB affair illustrates another important characteristic of cartel-like distributional coalitions. Like cartels of producers, these coalitions may be unstable and impermanent. Collusive deals worked out between members of distributional coalitions may be terminated when more profitable transactions present themselves. This is what happened in July 1984 when MPHB traded its 40 per cent share in UMBC for a 51 per cent controlling interest in the Malaysian-French Bank, thereby realising its long-standing objective of acquiring a bank to expand its access to liquidity.[30]

Privatisation and Asset Concentration

In recent years the Malaysian government has embarked on a policy of selling and transferring public enterprises to private interests. This policy, which is consistent with similar trends in other countries and is strongly favoured by such agencies as the World Bank, has the overall objective of encouraging greater investment in the private sector while reducing the public sector deficit.[31] In the Malaysian context of trusteeship, the policy of privatisation is almost certain to result in greater asset and wealth concentration in the hands of distributional coalitions. For example, public utilities are to be converted into private monopolies. Greater reliance on user-fees and ability-to-pay, without due regard to the equitable distribution of accompanying financial burdens, is bound to victimise lower-income groups. In the case of railways, the new owners are authorised to emphasise highly profitable real estate development at the expense of the less profitable rail traffic business. This shift in priorities will lower the economic welfare of rural and poorer households while increasing incomes and profits of those at the top.

The Malaysian strategy of privatisation has another serious limitation. The new entrepreneurs of the privatised enterprises are selected by ruling elites preferentially, first and foremost on political grounds. The award of a licence to launch a commercial television network, TV3, in August 1983 is a case in point. Fleet Group, the company awarded the licence by the cabinet, is the chief investment arm of UMNO, and its parent company, Fleet Holdings, is headed by the new Minister of Finance who is a close friend of the Prime Minister. Privatisation is often used as a method of rewarding loyalty for political service. In some cases, the existing networks are regrouped and reconstituted to fit the requirements of privatisation and take advantage of new opportunities for mutually enriching deals. For example, in September 1983, PNB, PERNAS and Guthrie's combined together with some private interests to form the Malaysian Overseas Investment Corporation (MOIC) to channel capital into investment projects in Fiji, the Maldives, etc. Yet Malaysia is a significant net importer of foreign capital.

Corruption as a Technique of Rent-seeking Behaviour

The cases reviewed earlier refer to examples of rent-seeking behaviour by various privileged and influential elite groups in the course of the ordinary decision-making process under the system of trusteeship. This review would be incomplete without considering an extreme technique of rent-seeking behaviour, viz. corruption, which is both elusive and universal.

What constitutes corruption is extremely difficult to specify. Alatas defines corruption as 'the subordination of public interests to private aims involving a violation of the norms of duty and welfare, accompanied by secrecy, betrayal, deception and a callous disregard for any consequences suffered by the public'.[32]If we accept his definition, then the illustrative case-studies above demonstrate that the Malaysian NEP trusteeship system is vulnerable to abuse by corrupt officials. Alatas, quoting the great fourteenth century Islamic scholar Ibni Khaldun, considered 'the root cause of corruption to be the passion for luxurious living within the ruling group'.[33]

Two of the most notorious examples of corruption among the Malaysian elites in recent times are the Bank Rakyat scandal of the mid-1970s and the Bank Bumiputera Finance scandal of 1983. Both of these are Bumiputera institutions, financed and owned by the government and intended to benefit the Malay community. The Bank Rakyat — People's Bank — began as a financial cooperative in 1954. Its main function was to help poor farmers and fishermen.[34] The Bank Bumiputera Finance is a subsidiary of the largest Malaysian bank, Bank Bumiputera, which was wholly-owned by the government.

In the Bank Rakyat scandal, the chairman of the board, the former Chief Minister of Selangor, and the managing director, were found guilty and imprisoned for embezzlement of public funds, criminal breach of trust and forging bank documents.[35] The Bank Bumiputera Finance scandal, at the time of writing in the summer of 1984, was still under formal investigation. These scandals have revealed various techniques of self-enrichment used by corrupt figures among which are the following:

Nominee Companies. The convicted managing director of the Bank Rakyat owned at least two such companies, Kwong Yik Nominees Sdn Bhd and Public Nominees Sdn Bhd on behalf of which he used to buy large blocks of shares paid for by Bank money. The Price Waterhouse report[36] revealed that the managing director had thus acquired 420,000 shares of the Kuala Lumpur-Kepong Amalgamated Ltd stock valued at $1.3 million and 151,000 shares in Malayan Banking Berhad worth $0.6 million, among numerous other similar acquisitions.[37] These transactions, spread over six years from 1972–77, were conducted on an on-going basis in collaboration with the chairman of the board and certain officials of the bank, including the chairman's lawyer son, who were all involved in the cover-up and forgery.

Unsecured Loans. A widely used, corrupt practice in the Bank Rakyat affair was the granting of large amounts of money to well-connected and influential politicians as unsecured loans with no collateral or proper documentation and processing. In one case, an executive councillor of the Kelantan state government borrowed a total of $1.26 million, including a loan of $710,000 for a company called Syarikat Perbadanan Perusahaan Pertanian of which he was a director. Another co-director took a further loan of $750,000. These loans ostensibly were to finance the 'purchase of green tobacco leaves by the company'.[38] In a land deal in Kajang, the brother of the chairman of the board, together with another businessman, took out an unsecured loan of $570,238, approved by the lawyer son of the chairman, in order to purchase three pieces of land. Subsequently, the land was resold to the bank for $751,000.[39]

Multiple Directorships and Interlocking Stockholding. The high concentration of corporate wealth and power in Malaysia is also promoted by multiple directorships and interlocking stockowner-ship deals which link the various distributional coalitions and networks.[40] These interlocks establish new cartels and monopolise corporate information. In turn, this access to information provides virtually unlimited opportunities for quasi-rents, self-enrichment through capital gains resulting from insider stock trading, contract awards, and other types of mutually profitable business deals. In addition, multiple directorships generate further personal income in the form of directors' and management fees as well as expense accounts. Malaysia does not have any anti-combines and unfair trade practice laws. As a result, conflicts of interest are common occurrences. An example of this practice was revealed in the Bank Rakyat corruption case. The convicted general manager was also the chairman of the board of the bank's subsidiaries which, on his instructions, were being charged excessive consultancy and management fees.[41]

Speculative Export of Capital. One of the important questions raised by the BMF Scandal is why a Bumiputera finance company should be involved in the speculative export of large amounts of capital (in this case up to $3 billion) from Malaysia, which itself is a significant net importer of capital. In particular, why should a subsidiary of a government-owned bank be involved in such transactions? This represents a serious breach of trust by those entrusted with the savings of ordinary citizens, not only because of the huge sums involved but also because it represents a continuing trend of corruption since the Bank Rakyat scandal.

Such a large amount of bad loans was bound to adversely affect the parent company, the Bank Bumiputera, wholly owned by the government. In September 1984 PETRONAS, the largest customer of Bank Bumiputera, was obliged to take over the Bank in a $2.4 billion 'rescue operation' to resolve the problem of the Hong Kong bad loans.[42] Since PETRONAS is a public enterprise with large profits derived from the sale of oil and gas, the effect of this transaction was to write off the bad debts of Malaysian distributional coalitions at the public's expense.

'Consultancy Fees', Commissions and Bribes. Both the Bank Bumiputera Finance and the Bank Rakyat cases revealed that directors and senior officials regularly collected 'consultancy fees', over and above emoluments, from their employers and clients for services rendered in negotiating and processing loans. In the case of the BMF scandal, it was disclosed in parliament that, between 1979–81, the chairman of Bank Bumiputera and four senior officers of the bank's Hong Kong subsidiary had accepted 'consultancy fees' amounting to HK$3.3 million from BMF.[43] In subsequent press reports of this affair, it was reported that such fees, sometimes called management fees, are common practice in Malaysia.[44] Earlier, in the Bank Rakyat scandal, Price Waterhouse had produced evidence of a fee-charging practice at the rate of 5 per cent for 'development management' and 10 per cent for 'management and financing' imposed on subsidiaries of the bank.[45] These were falsely justified and entered in the books as 'fees for services rendered by the directors, officers and employees of Bank Rakyat'.[46]

Before ending this section on corruption, it must be stated that the vast majority of the officials and managers of the NEP trusteeship system are honest and efficient and neither are greed and corruption limited to Malaysia. What is unique about the Malaysian system of NEP trusteeship is that it is promoting a non-competitive system in which the greatest benefits accrue to those who have the power to exercise collusion and influence-peddling. Those without power and connections tend to lose. Thus, under the system of NEP trusteeship a new type of inequality has emerged. Intra-ethnic inequality in income distribution is replacing the traditional inter-ethnic inequality.

Intra-ethnic Income Inequality

Tables 6.3 and 6.4, computed from the most recent data contained in the Mid-Term Review of the Fourth Malaysia Plan,[47] summarise *inter*-racial and *intra*-racial income disparities.

Looking at inter-racial disparities, it is evident that while the Malays as a group are still behind the Chinese, Indians and Others

Table 6.3: Income Distribution Trends among Races and Areas in Peninsular Malaysia, 1970–79

Races or Area	Ratio of median household incomes	
	1970	1979
Chinese/Malay	2.23	1.89
Indian/Malay	1.61	1.59
Others/Malay	1.38	1.68
Urban/Rural	1.90	1.62

Source: Table 3.8, MTR4MP, p. 94

Table 6.4: Income Distribution Trends within Specific Racial Groups and Areas in Peninsular Malaysia, 1970–79

Race or Area	Ratio of mean to median household income	
	1970	1979
Malay	1.43	1.50
Chinese	1.47	1.51
Indian	1.56	1.45
Others	3.25	3.47
All Races	1.59	1.59
Urban	1.61	1.62
Rural	1.43	1.49

Source: Table 3.8, MTR4MP, p. 94

on the basis of average household income, the disparity is gradually narrowing. In 1970 the ratio of Chinese/Malay median household income in Peninsular Malaysia was 2.23 while by 1979 it had dropped to 1.89. The Indian/Malay ratio also declined but at a much slower pace, while the Others/Malay ratio rose significantly (Table 6.3).

The equalisation trends revealed in Table 6.3 significantly understate the rate of progress toward equality because the household income fails to take account of inter-ethnic differences in the sizes of households. When household income *per capita* is calculated, the actual rate of equalisation of Malay/non-Malay disparity is seen to be occurring significantly faster during 1970–79. This is due to the fact the average Malay household is smaller than Chinese and Indian households.[48] Thus, when the ratio of median monthly household *per capita* income is computed, the Chinese/Malay disparity declined from 1.93 in 1970 to 1.69 in 1979. The Indian/Malay ratio remained stationary at about 1.5, while the All Races/Malay ratio declined from 1.31 to 1.28. These trends suggest that, while there is still some distance to go before inter-racial income disparities are totally eliminated, significant progress, in average terms, has been achieved in this direction since 1970.

However, the data in Table 6.4 indicate that, since 1970, a new form of income inequality had arisen in Malaysia. There has been increased inequality *within* given racial groups. This intra-group income inequality indicates that the richer households, controlled for race, have become richer in relation to lower-income families. This trend of increasing intra-group inequality is measured by taking the ratio of mean to median incomes, whereby a rising ratio reflects elitist income concentration. For the Malays, Chinese and Others the intra-group inequality worsened, but it improved significantly for the Indians, and remained stationary for All Races. Of the three principal races, the intra-group inequality rose fastest among the Malays. Also, such inequality increased marginally in urban areas and more significantly in rural areas.

The last set of data on intra-group inequalities confirms the theoretical expectation that the NEP trusteeship has rewarded selected members of 'distributional coalitions'. The rich got richer, more by collusion and patronage than by merit or competition. The trustees channelled public resources into wealth restructuring, while paying lip-service to poverty redressal, because the former created vast opportunities for self-enrichment. In the process, poverty redressal slowed down and, as a result, intra-group inequalities worsened.

Notes

1. Bruce Gale, *Politics and Public Enterprise in Malaysia*, Eastern Universities Press, Singapore, 1981, Appendix 4, pp. 224–8.
2. 'Govt agencies not under scrutiny', *Malaysia New Straits Times*, 11 April 1984, p. 1.
3. E.g. as in the case of MAJUTERNAK, the National Livestock Development Authority, which was closed down for mismanagement.
4. Regarding LPN subsidy abuses, see 'Rice millers ripping off millions in subsidies', *Malaysia New Straits Times*, 29 June 1983. On allegations that RISDA had misappropriated $130 million cess funds, in part to construct a luxury headquarters in Kuala Lumpur, see *New Sunday Times*, 28 August 1983.
5. Ozay Mehmet, 'Protection or Competition: The Challenge of Development Strategy in Malaysia', *Ilmu Masyarakat*, vol. 3, July–September, 1983, pp. 24–34.
6. Khor Kok Peng, *Recession and the Malaysian Economy*, Institut Masyarakat, Penang, 1983, p. 54.
7. 'The Political Economy of Public Enterprises in Malaysia' in *Malaysian Economy at the Crossroads: Policy Adjustment or Structural Transformation*, edited by Lim Lin Lean and Chee Peng Lim, Malaysian Economic Association, Kuala Lumpur, 1984, Table 2, p. 225.
8. 'How the SEDC firms fared in 1982', *Malaysia New Straits Times*, 4 March 1984.
9. This term is borrowed from Mancur Olson. See his recent book: *The Rise and Decline of Nations*, Yale University Press, New Haven, Conn., 1982.
10. The defence forces chief, Gen. Tan Sri Ghazali Seth is a cousin of the former prime minister Tun Hussein Onn, whose brother, Datuk Jaafar Onn was the deputy chief of the army. Tunku Abdul Rahman, Malaysia's first prime minister, was the uncle of the then defence chief Tunku Osman Jiawa. In January 1984, Maj. General Hashim Mohamad Ali, who is the prime minister Mahathir's brother-in-law, was appointed deputy chief of the army. See 'Malaysia: Out of step. . .', *Far Eastern Economic Review*, 12 January 1984, p. 40.
11. For such studies, see Tan Tat Wai, *Income Distribution and Determination in West Malaysia*, Oxford University Press, Kuala Lumpur, 1982, esp. Ch. 8; Lim Mah Hui, *Ownership and Control of the One Hundred Largest Corporations in Malaysia*, Oxford University Press, Singapore, 1981, esp. Ch. 5.
12. See 'An arm's-length stance on business activities', *Far Eastern Economic Review*, 20 October 1983, p. 50.
13. KLSE *Handbook*.
14. 'Fleet and Philips in high-technology joint venture', *Malaysia New Straits Times*, 13 February 1984, p. 17.
15. FELDA *Annual Report* 1981, p. 20.
16. 'Nestlé for restructuring', *Malaysia New Straits Times*, 23 September 1983.
17. G. Means, *Malaysian Politics*, Hodder and Stoughton, London, 1970.
18. See Ch. 5, pp. 115–17.
19. See the publication, *Antah Holdings Sdn Bhd*, Kuala Lumpur, no date.
20. The biggest money-making company, Securicor (M) Sdn Bhd, provides guards and security personnel. It is a joint venture with Securicor International Ltd., of England with Antah holding a 51 per cent majority share.

154   *The Social Costs of Trusteeship*

21. 'Antah comes to the market', *Far Eastern Economic Review*, 20 October 1983, p. 94.
22. 'The End of an Affair', *Asiaweek*, 13 April 1984, p. 44.
23. Permodalan Nasional Berhad, *Annual Report* 1982, p. 3 and 1980, p. 10.
24. See the PNB's publication, *Policy Guidelines on Investments*, para. 7(ii), p. 17 (no date).
25. PNB *Annual Report* 1982, p. 27.
26. 'Anatomy of a Crisis', *Malaysian Business*, 1 April 1984, pp. 11–13.
27. 'Multi-faceted conglomerate has 'sogo-sosha aspirations' *Asian Business*, November 1982, pp. 42–7.
28. Toh Kin Woon, *The State in Economic Development: A Case Study of Malaysia's New Economic Policy*, PhD Thesis, University of Malaya, January 1982, pp. 244–50.
29. See *New Sunday Times*, 22 March 1981, p. 7 and *Malaysia New Straits Times*, 23 March 1981, p. 7 carrying statements by the UMNO and MCA youth wing leaders.
30. See 'Why UMBC was Swapped', *Sunday Star*, 8 July 1984, p.5.
31. MTR4MP, pp. 22–3.
32. Syed Hussein Alatas, *The Sociology of Corruption, The Nature, Function, Causes and Prevention of Corruption*, Times Books International, Singapore, 1980, p. 12.
33. Ibid., p. 9.
34. Bruce Gale, *Policies and Public Enterprise in Malaysia*, pp. 176–9.
35. 'Calling debtors to account', *Far Eastern Economic Review*, 13 July 1979, pp. 69–72.
36. See the special report commissioned by the Malaysian Government, *Lapuran Price Waterhouse & Co., Final Report, vol. I, 1979,* para. 15.3. Also, see the White Paper: Malaysia, *Kedudukan Bank Rakyat*, Government Printer, Kuala Lumpur, 1979.
37. Price Waterhouse, *Final Report*, paras. 15.3–15.23.
38. Ibid., section on the Kota Bharu Branch, para. 21, p. 12.
39. Ibid., section on the Kuala Lumpur Branch, paras. 14–27, pp. 11–18.
40. Lim Mah Hui, *Ownership and Control,* esp. Ch. 7.
41. Price Waterhouse report, *Interim Report*, para. 85, p. 53.
42. *Malaysian Digest*, vol. 15, no. 18, 30 September 1984.
43. Lim Kit Siang, *The BMF Scandal*, Petaling Jaya, 3.12.1983, p. 9.
44. See the press statement of BMF general manager, Ibrahim Jaafar, as reported in the *Malaysia New Straits Times*, 'BMF GM denies he received fees', 14 October 1983, p. 1.
45. Price Waterhouse report, *Interim Report*, para. 87, p. 54.
46. Ibid., para. 91, p. 57.
47. MTR4MP, Table 3.8, p. 94.
48. 4MP, Table 4.3, p. 75.

PART FOUR: PROSPECTS AND ALTERNATIVES

7 SUMMING UP: PROBLEMS, PROSPECTS AND ALTERNATIVES

Introduction

In this final chapter we summarise the main conclusions of the study and examine some of the principal policy issues, alternatives and prospects of Malaysian development. As 1990 draws near the central question of development strategy in Malaysia is what to do about the NEP: terminate it? extend it? or redesign it?

The single most important conclusion of the study is that, despite ample resources and rapid growth, the strategy of NEP trusteeship has failed to eradicate poverty, and indeed many of the adopted policies have tended to perpetuate and reproduce it. Trusteeship has resulted in a very rapid process of wealth accumulation under the direct control of the trustees themselves. These consequences follow from *biased decision-making*, concentrated in the hands of the trustees. They have taken advantage of their positions, promoting self-enrichment through rent-seeking behaviour and other non-competitive rewards accruing to 'distributional coalitions'.[1] These coalitions have emerged as an increasing deadweight burden on the Malaysian economy, augmenting its non-competitive aspects. We shall now illustrate the emergence of a non-competitive economy under the NEP trusteeship, using a simple marginal productivity framework.

The Analytics of Trusteeship: How Quasi-Rents Arise

The central feature of development by trusteeship is *control* exercised by trustees on behalf of nominal beneficiaries. This control extends over economic decision-making, including resource allocation and, most importantly, over the distribution of economic rewards. Concentration of control gives rise to cartel-like networks seeking quasi-rents as unearned income.[2]

Production and Distribution

Under trusteeship, production is organised on the same rules of efficiency as a competitive system: Labour (L), Capital and Technology (K), and Land (N) are utilised to produce output (Q) within a production function:

$$Q = F(L,K,N) \tag{1}$$

and an increment of output, dQ, is derived from additional increments of inputs multiplied by their respective marginal products:

$$dQ = f_l \cdot dL + f_k \cdot dK + f_n \cdot dN \tag{2}$$

The first condition of efficiency requires that the value of marginal products be equated with their marginal cost. This ensures that profits are maximised.

Profits, π, are simply the excess of total revenue, TR, over total cost, TC, which, under perfectly competitive conditions, is the sum of the cost of all inputs utilised in the production process. Profits, too, represent a return on the risk-taking entrepreneurial function. As a result, the value of output is completely divided among all the inputs contributing to it:

$$\pi = TR - TC \tag{3}$$

$$Y = wL + rK + nN + \pi \tag{4}$$

where Y is the monetary value of output, Q, priced at p:

$$Y = p \cdot Q \tag{5}$$

In practice, this competitive system has too many inherent weaknesses to be applicable. There are 'market imperfections' generating economic exploitation. In particular, there may be monopoly or monopsony powers which enable those with such powers to fix prices and corner markets to their own advantage. Likewise, cartel-like networks with privileged access to vital information on prices, supplies and market conditions may practise collusion.[3] As a result, the distribution of economic rewards may not conform to equation (4). Some inputs may be under-compensated (i.e. paid less than their marginal products) while others are over-compensated. Thus, an increment of income, dY, may contain unearned margins in the form of quasi-rent:

$$dY = dE + dZ \tag{6}$$

where dE refers to an increment of earned income and dZ to

cumulated unearned margins from quasi-rents. More specifically, assuming that labour is under-compensated while capital and land are over-compensated:

$$dE = (1 - \lambda) \, \delta w/\delta L \cdot dL + (1 + \phi) \, \delta r/\delta K \cdot dK$$
$$+ (1 + \psi) \, \delta n/\delta N \cdot dN \tag{7}$$

and

$$dZ = \lambda \cdot \delta w/\delta L \cdot dL = \phi \cdot \delta r/\delta K \cdot dK + \psi \cdot \delta n/\delta N \cdot dN \tag{8}$$

where λ, ϕ, and ψ refer to marginal quasi-rents.

Equation (8) states that the quasi-rents received by owners of land and capital exactly match the under-compensation of labour. In other words, there is transfer of value-added from workers to the owners of capital and land.

Quasi-rents under Trusteeship

Quasi-rents can occur under any imperfectly competitive economic system dominated by oligopolies and cartels who are able to charge 'administered prices', and powerful lobbies and special interest groups who likewise charge 'transaction costs' for services rendered as middlemen. These administered prices and transaction costs are passed on to primary resource owners (primarily the unorganised workers and peasants) on the one hand, and to final consumers on the other. As has been argued by Olson, they represent a powerful cause of the phenomenon of stagflation in industrialised countries.[4]

Administered prices and middlemen transaction costs are widespread in Malaysia. They have become institutionalised under the NEP trusteeship which has centralised economic decision-making and actively encouraged the emergence of closely interlocking 'distributional coalitions'. Many retail prices as well as wages are controlled by the government. Statutory bodies enjoy monopoly or monopsony powers. Members of the distributional coalitions regularly collect commissions, fees and middlemen margins as transaction costs for arranging contracts and deals. These transaction costs are received in the form of a percentage, lump-sum cash or payment in kind. The NEP trusteeship has legitimised and considerably extended this non-competitive system of rewards accruing as quasi-rents to the various distributional coalitions.

The social costs of these quasi-rents are passed on to the

unorganised and politically weak owners of primary resources such as peasants or female factory workers. Thus, the wages of tappers on estates (Chapter 2) or of migrant industrial workers in labour-intensive industries (Chapter 4) are maintained at or below subsistence levels, significantly below the value of their marginal productivity. Similarly, peasants whose lands are expropriated for development as industrial estates or urban housing projects may be provided with inadequate compensation (e.g. the case of Thean Teik in Penang). On the other hand, surpluses enrich corporate interests and their associated distributional coalitions. The latter also derive quasi-rents from subsidies granted to owners of capital, as tax write-offs and credits or as low-interest loans, ostensibly to accelerate industrialisation and modernisation.

Thus, under the NEP trusteeship, equation (4) no longer applies. By formal or informal methods, the trustees determine the marginal rewards accruing to L, K, and N. Thus,

$$f_l = \overline{w} \neq w$$
$$f_k = \overline{r} \neq r$$
$$f_n = \overline{n} \neq n \tag{9}$$

What are the policy instruments by which the trustees can determine these rewards? They include the power to resist land reform, to control prices, to maintain a cheap labour policy and to mobilise savings. Resisting land reform keeps peasants and smallholders in poverty (Chapters 2 and 3). The cheap labour policy, inherited from the colonial era, reproduces poverty on plantations where real wages have declined since 1960 despite a productivity gain of 2¼ times and where there is now increasing reliance on imported Indonesian labour willing to work at subsistence wages. The cheap labour policy is also practised by FELDA, in respect of its own settlers, who are encouraged to accumulate large debts against future incomes, reminiscent of the hated *padi kunca* system, as well as through its reliance on exploitative labour contractors. Migrant industrial workers, especially female factory operatives in labour-intensive industries, are similarly exploited (Chapter 4) by cheap labour policies implemented to attract foreign investment to the Malaysian industrial estates.

Forced Savings

A major policy instrument successfully used by the NEP trustees for enlarging the size of quasi-rents has been forced savings. These are imposed on workers to depress their current consumption in favour of savings which increased from 21.6 per cent of GNP in 1970 to 27.2 per cent in 1980 (Table 1.1). Forced savings through statutory payroll deductions (such as EPF, SOCSO), numerous institutionalised pension funds and savings associations, as well as through Islamic banking, are all controlled by distributional coalitions (Chapters 5 and 6). They have helped to mobilise and channel a rising flow of domestic savings into wealth restructuring and corporate asset formation under the direct control of trustees. FELDA's emergence as one of the top corporate entities in Malaysia is one of the clearest examples of successful manipulation of forced savings by the controlling trustees in their dedication to achieving corporate growth and self-aggrandisement at the expense of the economic welfare of its settlers.

Cheap labour policies, forced savings and resistance to land reform are extremely powerful economic instruments in the hands of trustees for generating quasi-rents and wealth concentration. To generalise, suppose that a community consists of two groups: trustees, who control economic decision-making, and workers. The trustees derive their income, Y^T, in the form of quasi-rents, while the workers earn theirs, Y^L, from selling their labour to employers as input into the production process:

$$Y = Y^T + Y^L \tag{10}$$

$$Y^T = y^t(Z, A) \tag{11}$$

$$Y^L = y^l(L) \tag{12}$$

Equation (11) reflects the fact that trustees have two sources of income: quasi-rents, Z, as explained in equations (6)−(8), and an additional return from assets, A, under their effective control.

Asset formation (and redistribution) is a positive function of the national savings rate, s:

$$A = a(s) \tag{13}$$

where

$$s = S/Y \tag{14}$$

and

$$S = S^T + S^L \tag{15}$$

However, the sources of savings and the behaviour of the two groups differ significantly. The trustees' savings accrue from their control of decision-making and are speculatively utilised. They rise and fall with the expected rate of return. Thus a good deal of these savings may be exported abroad for quick gains (e.g. the BMF Hong Kong scandal) or used for speculative capital gains on the stock exchange in Kuala Lumpur or elsewhere. The savings of workers are forced savings, collected as payroll deductions at the expense of current consumption:

$$S = s\,(i) \qquad\qquad s_i > 0 \qquad\qquad\qquad (16)$$

$$S = s\,(C) \qquad\qquad s_c < 0 \qquad\qquad\qquad (17)$$

where i is the interest rate determining the expected rate of return and C is the workers' current consumption.

Thus there is a second source of conflicting interests between the trustees and workers centred on the temporal allocation of income between savings and consumption. For example, a cheap labour policy may not only be a source of quasi-rents for the trustees, as explained in equation (7); it is also a necessary condition for depressing the current consumption of workers in order to increase the future speculative gains of the trustees as shown in equations (11)–(15).

Failure of the 'Trickle-down' Theory

This theory predicts that high and sustained rates of economic growth automatically lead to poverty reduction and balanced development, benefiting an ever-widening circle of the population. It is a theory which has long been adopted by the Malaysian trustees. Furthermore, since 1970 the Malaysian GNP has grown very impressively and during 1970–80 there was a 60 per cent increase in real *per capita* income. Despite this impressive growth performance, the strategy of trusteeship failed to achieve even its own targets in poverty reduction. Yet there has been a rapid acceleration in wealth concentration in terms of corporate assets as well as human capital and other forms of wealth.

The NEP trusteeship does not contradict the marginal productivity theory. The trustees ensure that production conforms to efficiency criteria, but they deliberately interfere with the market forces in resource allocation (e.g. job quotas). However, their dominant influence is over the distribution of income which, as a result, bears little relationship to productivity.

The emergence of an increasingly non-competitive economy under the NEP trusteeship implies that the trickle-down process may be aborted by a *zero-sum game*. The trustees may choose to divert the proceeds of income growth into further corporate expansion and wealth accumulation under their own control, not only at the expense of workers' current consumption, but also at the expense of investment in raising the productivity of the poor. In a dynamic sense, the trustees may effectively manipulate the income share of the peasants and workers, by means of cheap labour policies, forced savings and resistance to land reform, so as always to keep their consumption at subsistence levels.

Of course it may be argued that the Malaysian system of trusteeship requires a longer period of time to demonstrate its trickle-down process. This argument is suspect on two important grounds. First, the length of 'required' time is unspecified. For instance, in neighbouring Singapore, it has required a much shorter period of time. In Malaysia, however, it is being offset, among other things, by massive capital exports for speculative purposes which is contrary to the classical assumption that capitalist accumulation leads to future growth through 'ploughing back' of profits and savings. Secondly, it is evident that Malaysian development by trusteeship is petrifying the control of trustees and the quasi-rents of 'distributional coalitions'. In fact, the trusteeship system has all the power and capacity for self-reproduction. For example, the Malaysian university system and the government scholarship policy tend to be manipulated by the influential and powerful households to prepare their children for the next generation of trustees. Extension of the NEP, in its original form, beyond 1990 will almost certainly petrify the control of trustees and further retard the trickling-down process.

Zero-Sum Game under the NEP Trusteeship

The evidence reviewed in this study leads to the conclusion that the Malaysian trusteeship fits a *Zero-Sum Economic Game*[5] in which the trustees have gained at the expense of the losers, the large number of poor families who have remained poor.

Yet development by trusteeship is not inherently in conflict with poverty redressal and a more egalitarian distribution strategy. The trustees who control resource allocation and, in particular, determine distribution policies may, if they so choose, adopt wage and income policies effectively providing additional purchasing power to the poor households to raise their incomes to the official poverty-level-of-income.

Is this likely to decelerate the growth rate? Theoretically, it may appear that tranfers in aid of the poor may be at the expense of investment and growth. In fact, however, such transfers could actually augment effective demand and accelerate growth to the extent that they were financed by diverting funds from such unproductive uses as speculative capital exports.

Let us now give a hypothetical illustration to clarify the implications of such cash transfers (Table 7.1).

Suppose a community is made up of ten individuals, divided into three socio-economic groups: two rich (R), two mildly poor (MP), and six hard-core poor (HCP). Initially, total income (Y_0) is $100 which is unequally distributed in the ratio of 6:2.2:1.8. The average *per capita* income for the community is $10, but there is a wide variation around it, since the average income of the two rich is $30, $11 for the two MP and just $3 for the six HCP. In fact, the last figure is below the exogeneously determined poverty-level income of $4. As a result of this initial unequal distribution, there are not only large absolute disparities but also relative disparities ranging from 2.7 for R/MP to 10 for R/HCP.

Following planned economic growth, let us assume that the community's aggregate income rises by an increment of $10. The question which we focus on is how is this incremental income to be distributed among the three groups? It can be done in an elitist or egalitarian way, both options being subject to the discretion of trustees as decision-makers.

Even under an elitist distribution of 7:2:1, all three groups experience rising absolute average *per capita* income, along with a 10 per cent overall increase from $10 to $11. Of course, the rich gain the most while the hard-core poor gain the least and as a result, income disparities widen. The elite may ask — why worry, since all groups are experiencing improved incomes? Of course the reason is that economic growth — which is as high as 10 per cent — is failing to cure poverty *because* the rich are getting richer.

Alternatively, a more egalitarian pattern of distribution, 1:3:6, may be adopted by trustees who genuinely wish to eliminate

Table 7.1: A Hypothetical Illustration of Alternative Distribution of Income Growth

Item	Symbol	Total	Socio-economic groups R / P = MP + HCP				Y/N	Average				R/P	Disparities	
			R	P	MP	HCP		R/N	P/N	MP/N	HCP/N		R/MP	R/HCP
Population	N	10	2	8	2	6								
Initial Income	Y_0	$100	60	40	22	18	10	30	5	11	3	6	2.7	10
Poverty Level of Income	PLI	$4												
Subsequent Income	Y_1	$110												
Income Growth	$\triangle Y$	$10												

Distribution Patterns:

	R	MP	HCP	R	P	MP	HCP	Y/N	R/N	P/N	MP/N	HCP/N	R/P	R/MP	R/HCP
i. Elitist	7	2	1	67	43	24	19	11	33.5	5.375	12	3.2	6.2	2.75	10.5
ii. Balanced Growth	1	3	6	61	49	25	24	11	30.5	6.125	12.5	4	5.0	2.4	7.6

poverty by means of a balanced growth strategy (Table 7.1, last row). Thus, they would raise the consumption of the poor at the expense of incremental wealth accumulation of the rich. Of course, the *per capita* income will still be $11, but now relative disparities will narrow significantly. Even more importantly, the hard-core poor will have an average income of $4 thus breaking out of poverty, providing that there was no population growth, in the meantime, to add to the size of HCP.

Both patterns of distribution would be compatible with a system of economic trusteeship. It ultimately depends on how the trustees wish to allocate the benefits of income growth among the three groups. In Malaysia, with its highly favourable resource-endowment and very impressive growth performance, large-scale poverty can be eradicated speedily if the trustees wish it. Conversely, its persistence evidently stems directly from a lack of commitment on the part of the trustees to eradicate it.

Policy Choices and Alternatives

In comparison with some other resource-constrained developing countries and with some of its densely populated neighbours, poverty eradication in Malaysia is considerably more feasible and can be accomplished relatively speedily. Furthermore, given Malaysia's strategy of development by trusteeship, in which income shares are primarily determined by the decisions of trustees rather than by competitive market forces, poverty eradication rests first and foremost upon political will to increase the income share of the poor households relatively to the rest of the population.

If the trustees were willing, there is no reason why poverty in Malaysia could not be eradicated within a relatively short time. What would be some of the main policy measures required for such an approach? Only some general outlines of reformist action can be specified here, since more specific steps were indicated, explicitly or implicitly, in earlier parts of this book.

Labour Market and Manpower Policies

The principal policy target ought to be termination of the cheap labour policy in the plantation sector and, simultaneously, the phasing-out of the low-wage policy in the modern sector. Higher wages need not adversely affect the international competitiveness of Malaysian exports because the data clearly show that labour costs are too small a fraction of productivity. Low wages essentially make for excessively large profit margins and returns to capital.

At the same time, effective measures and policies need to be implemented to raise the productivity of the poor including the working poor. Investments in skill training, and technical and vocational education enhance the income-earning capacity of workers while also raising the level of output. It is not sufficient merely to expand the number of jobs (as happened with labour-intensive industrialisation under the Pioneer Industries scheme) because they may turn out to be unskilled and low-paying jobs yielding poverty-level incomes. There must be *skill deepening*, (as happened in Singapore, South Korea and Japan) enhancing the quality and productivity of workers. A rising labour share of income requires *both* more job opportunities *and* higher wages. A freer trade union movement, empowered to organise, strike and bargain for better working conditions, is also essential to counter-vail the powers of management as well as the cartel-like powers of 'distributional coalitions'.

In so far as the formation of human capital through the higher education system is concerned, elitist scholarships and privileged accessibility should be phased out and replaced by user cost principles. Student aid should be restricted exclusively to qualified but financially deprived students regardless of race.

Regulation of Technology and Capital Imports

In the past, the strategy of Malaysian industrialisation has encouraged capital-intensive technology imports. In fact, foreign capital has been subsidised through tax exemptions, credits and accelerated depreciation allowances. All of these incentives have actively promoted substitution of capital for domestic labour thereby reducing both the quantity and the quality of job creation. As a result, retained income as a percentage of value-added has been reduced in direct proportion to net payments to foreign capital and technology imports. In future, a more socially appro-priate policy would regulate capital and technology imports from the standpoint of maximising the ratio of retained income to value added.

Micro-planning and Project Appraisal

Regulating capital and technology imports as indicated above would require major shifts in the Malaysian approach to planning. In the past this approach has been heavily macro-economic, emphasising aggregate relationships and ignoring specific issues such as how particular projects get selected and the impacts of given subsidy programmes. These specific decisions have been dominated by distributional coalitions pursuing their own special interests in order to bias resource allocation in their favour (Chapter 6). Currently, the Malaysian government is following a *Look East* policy,[6] attempting to borrow from the Japanese and South Korean development experience. One specific lesson which could be learned is the Korean emphasis on micro-planning and policy management. For example, the Korean Development Institute would provide an excellent model for re-orienting the Malaysian Economic Planning Unit away from aggregate, macro-planning toward evaluations of specific projects (both ex-ante and ex-post), impact studies of particular subsidy programmes and publishing the results on a regular basis as a contribution to improving the efficiency and equity of economic policy.

Competition Policy and Privatisation

At the present time, Malaysia does not have any anti-trust laws and unfair trade practices regulations providing standards for fair competition. In this environment, the Malaysian government is currently attempting to pursue a privatisation policy. However desirable it may be to lessen the degree of state capitalism and the deficit/GNP ratio, there are great risks that privatisation might convert public monopolies into private monopolies, charging excessive rates and realising inordinately high profit margins. Such undesirable results can be avoided, partly by enacting clear and legally enforcible rules for fair trade practices and partly by encouraging the establishment of countervailing consumer watch-dog groups. Such groups would not only protect the general public from monopolies but also from distributional coalitions collecting quasi-rents.

Land Reform and Rural Development

Land reform aimed at the consolidation of uneconomic holdings in both the rubber and padi sectors is an indispensable prerequisite for rural development in Malaysia. Such a reform would raise the productivity of land and the incomes of padi farmers and small-holders. It would also release considerable labour now blocked in marginal cultivation in these activities and maintained by means of inefficiently-administered subsidy programmes (Chapter 3).

As an additional strategy, small-scale rural industrialisation should be encouraged with incentives equally attractive to those offered to capital-intensive, large foreign firms that reward capital at the expense of labour. Evidence from other developing countries shows that small-scale rural industrialisation is relatively labour-intensive.[7] In Malaysia there is a further long-term trend in favour of shifting to rural industrial development. Traditional farming and artisanal fishing, heavily subsidised in the past, are uneconomic and will become increasingly so in the future as diets change and as the domestic terms of trade deteriorate further. Therefore, policies should encourage reallocation of resources into alternative productive uses, rather than blocking them in marginal and uneconomic employment. Encouragement of rural industries makes more economic sense than subsidies for traditional agriculture experiencing structural decline.

A Need-based Social Safety Net

One specific anti-poverty proposal worth careful consideration by the trustees is a National Dividend for poor households. The basic idea is to give a cash supplement to each poor household with no strings attached, in an effort to help push their income toward the poverty-level income. Of course, the National Dividend would be available to all poor households, irrespective of race. It should be regularly and strictly monitored to ensure that it is limited only to the needy and given directly to them with no intermediaries. The modalities and consequences of such a 'social safety net' have already been illustrated with a hypothetical example above and in Table 7.1.

How could the National Dividend be financed? The most logical method would be to impose a capital gains tax and use the proceeds to finance the National Dividend. At the present time Malaysia has no capital gains tax, which tends to enrich speculators and rich rent-seeking middlemen. Alternatively, or additionally, the National Dividend could be financed by reforming the ASN to incorporate this proposal. At the moment the ASN is restrictive in two important ways. First, it is restricted to Malays and secondly, participation in it depends on the ability-to-pay principle. As a result, even the poor Malays cannot afford to participate and many who do are often obliged to cash in their units at par value, in effect cross-subsidising other participants. There is no logical reason to maintain these restrictive aspects. Poverty in Malaysia is no longer as severely limited to Malays as at the outset of the NEP. The wealth of the country should be made available to all, and the needy of all races should be provided with a fair and equal share.

The main objection against the National Dividend proposal is that it represents a welfare 'hand-out' and it is, therefore, likely to discourage productive work. However, this argument is relevant only in a competitive economy in which income shares are derived from productive employment and earnings. Under the Malaysian system of trusteeship, income shares are not competitively determined. For example, elites do not derive their income share through productive employment. As far as the argument that equitable distribution may conflict with the growth objective is concerned, we have seen that resource allocation under the trusteeship system has not prevented wasteful and unproductive uses of scarce resources.

Permanent Protection or Fair Competition[8]

Beyond the provision of a National Dividend, based on need irrespective of race, it would be timely to phase out protectionism in favour of more competition in the Malaysian economy. This would be essential to check the growing power of 'distributional coalitions' and cartel-like networks who have cornered economic planning and policy under the NEP for self-enrichment. 'Competition' should not be taken to mean the text-book model of perfect competition in which only cost-efficient and price-competitive firms survive and where factors are always remunerated according to their productivity, merit and performance. The real world is far too imperfect and public policy, including development policy, cannot be designed on impractical ideals.

Of the many limitations of the textbook model of perfect competition, there is one which is of special relevance to the Malaysian case. The initial socio-economic structure may be extremely unequal. In particular, the ownership and control of productive resources may be so skewed that any competition, under conditions *as they are*, would merely aggrandise those already entrenched in wealth and power. For example, we saw that at the outset of the NEP the Malay share of corporate equity was virtually non-existent, and their stock of human capital was not much better. Therefore, in this sense it can be stated that the NEP was historically justifiable on the basis that affirmative action programmes promote fairness in the *terms of competition*.

But the same argument is clearly subject to a sunset clause. The terms of competition ultimately must be declared fair and protectionism must be phased out. If this is not done,[9] the risk of permanent protectionism is economic bankruptcy under mounting deficits and subsidies resulting from institutionalised quasi-rents and other non-competitive rewards which enrich elites. The evidence presented in this study strongly indicates that the Malaysian system of trusteeship is now at a crucial crossroads. On the one hand, there is institutionalised elitism with mass poverty reproduction as a necessary condition. On the other, there is more competition based on fairer distribution of economic and social benefits available to all.

Justice as Fairness and Compensating Benefits

According to John Rawls[10] justice as fairness requires that, if the original state (regarding income and wealth distribution) is unequal, the interests of the relatively disadvantaged should be safeguarded by means of *compensating benefits*. In the context of the Malaysian NEP, these benefits were necessary to equalise the terms of competition between the Malays and non-Malays. Since 1970, the NEP trusteeship has been very successful in restructuring the ownership and control of corporate and human capital assets although new forms of intra-group inequalities have emerged and poverty reduction has not been as successful as wealth restructuring.

Accordingly, future state assistance should be directed only to poverty reduction. Subsidies and grants to restructure wealth can no longer be justified under the original argument that the terms of inter-racial competition are unfair and unequal for Malays as a whole. Under the system of trusteeship they own and control virtually one-third of the corporate assets. Malay students receive most of the government scholarships and university places. Yet trusteeship policies have failed to eliminate poverty in Malaysia. For this reason, future compensating benefits should be tied strictly to poverty reduction. State assistance to redress poverty, given under the National Dividend proposal, should be provided selectively, only for the needy, rather than on the basis of ethnic membership. The rationale of such selectively distributed state assistance is to raise the productivity of the poor and the needy toward levels of parity with their more fortunate fellow-citizens. Once the productivity of the poor has been effectively raised through acquisition of human capital, land, corporate equity or other forms of income-yielding assets, they too, would be taken off the list of those needing state assistance. They would become self-reliant citizens earning their own way without state subsidies.

This system of need-based, selectively-provided compensating benefits for the poor to raise their productivity does not mean that state assistance ought to be subject to a sunset clause. On the contrary, it would exist on a permanent basis since there would always be disadvantaged citizens as individuals and households who move up and down the socio-economic ladder. The scope of such assistance would be far less, and it would be far more defensible on grounds of social justice, than the existing NEP trusteeship of wealth concentration at the cost of persistent mass poverty.

Notes

1. Mancur Olson, *The Rise and Decline of Nations*, Yale University Press, New Haven, Conn., 1982.
2. Strictly defined, quasi-rents refer to factor returns, over and above their transfer prices, due to unique skills or attributes which cannot be employed in alternative uses. This concept is applied to the Malaysian trustees who, as with any ruling elite, would, of course, claim that they are uniquely suited to the trusteeship role.
3. Olson, *Rise and Decline*, esp. pp. 196–202.
4. Ibid.
5. Lester C. Thurow, *The Zero Sum Society*, Penguin Books, New York, 1981.
6. *Mid-Term Review of the Fourth Malaysia Plan*, p. 25.
7. D. Anderson and M. W. Leiserson, 'Rural Nonfarm Employment in Developing Countries', *Economic Development and Cultural Change*, vol. 28, no. 2, January 1980, pp. 227–48.
8. This section is a revised version of O. Mehmet, 'Protection or Competition: The Emerging Challenge of Development Strategy in Malaysia', *Ilmu Masyarakat*, vol. 3, July–September 1983, pp. 24–34.
9. Recently some prominent politicians in Malaysia have argued that the protectionist NEP policies may be extended beyond 1990. See the statement by Musa Hitam, the Deputy Prime Minister: 'New Strategy may be needed for '90s: Musa', *Business Times*, 20 June 1983.
10. J. Rawls, *A Theory of Justice*, Harvard University Press, Cambridge, Mass., 1971, pp. 14–15.

INDEX

182 *Index*

*For Product Safety Concerns and Information please contact
our EU representative GPSR@taylorandfrancis.com Taylor & Francis
Verlag GmbH, Kaufingerstraße 24, 80331 München, Germany*

T - #0052 - 160425 - C0 - 216/138/11 [13] - CB - 9780415608886 - Gloss Lamination